Miracle Cures and Better Health

Beyond the Teachings of Hulda Clark

Richard Wachter

Robert D. Reed Publishers * Bandon, OR

Robert D. Reed Publishers
P.O. Box 1992
Bandon, OR 97411
E-mail: cleone@rdrpublishers.com
Website: www.rdrpublishers.com

Cover Designer: Cleone Reed
E-Book Designer: Susan Leonard
Paperback Formatting: Cleone Reed

2014 eBook ISBN: 978-1-934759-90-5
2023 Softcover ISBN: 979-8-88757-280-2

Library of Congress Control Number: 2023931825

Designed and Formatted in the United States of America

Disclaimer by the Publisher: The use of information provided in this book and the website links are at the reader's own risk. All of the information contained within is offered on an informational basis only. The Publisher assumes no responsibility for the readers' decisions. None of the content of this book is intended by the Publisher to be a substitute for professional medical advice, diagnosis, or treatment. If you choose to utilize any information provided in this book, you do so solely at your own risk.

IS IT REALLY A CURE?

"The word cure in the title was chosen, rather than treatment, because it is scientifically accurate.

"When the true cause of an illness has been found and, by removing it, the illness can be stopped or prevented, a true cure has also been found. When the cause is not found but the symptoms can be removed, helpful as this, you have only found a treatment. My research was a search for the causes of disease, how they might be removed, and whether their removal would lead to relief from the disease. I did not search merely for relief from the disease as most regular research does."

~ From Hulda Clark's many books.

ACKNOWELDGMENTS

To my family, immediate and extended,
in-laws and outlaws,
I am you!

My older brother Joe opened my mind
when I was young,
and he continues to keep me open
to new ideas and concepts
as we age.
I am forever in his debt.

My business partner and friend,
David Norgren,
made it possible for me
to do the research
and carry on Hulda Clark's work.

Contents

ABOUT THE AUTHOR

Richard Wachter

- Born: Yankton, South Dakota, 1944
- Family moved to California in 1955
- California State at Los Angeles Psychology Dept. Until 1966

- Drafted into US Army in 1966
- Viet Nam 1967 and 1968
- Motion picture industry from 1968 to 1999 as electronic engineer
- Beachcomber 1999 to present
- Near-death experience 2001; took up Hulda Clark books and studied her protocols, which saved my life; started helping other people.

How I got started with health care: 2001 MD Doctor Fariu told me I would die that night as my platelet count had dropped to danger levels and they had no idea what was wrong with me and had nothing to help me avoid death. As I left the hospital pondering this, I drove to my post office box to see if I had any mail. There was a slip saying I had a box to pick up at the main post office. I didn't want to go home so I went and picked up the box. It was from my older brother Joe with a note saying, "Try this." Inside I found Hulda Clarks' book *The Cure for All Diseases* and an early bio-wave frequency generator. I went to the beach and sat on the sand with the generator running while thinking about dying that night and how to tell my family. After a while I noticed I was feeling better. I drove home still zapping away, turned on the

TV, and fell asleep. I woke up the next morning feeling better than I had in months. I was alive. I drove back to the hospital and walked into Dr. Fariu office; he saw me and almost fell off of his chair and said, "You are alive?" I said, "I think so and I feel great." He sent me to the lab. I brought the readout back to him and he said, "You have had a miracle." I told him that the miracle was the little black box. I completely cured the arthritis that had plagued me for many years and the leukemia that it had caused. My success was so apparent to everyone who knew me that I was besieged with requests to help other people. Better Health Research Centre was created. I have helped thousands of people cure all sorts of disease.

INTRODUCTION

I grew up in a small town in the center of North America; land-locked farm country. I did not see an ocean until I was ten years old. Always an avid reader, my favorite author was Jack London; his tales of the South Pacific made me dream of oceans and sailing and especially ISLANDS. I became totally enamored of the island as the ideal place to live: a sandy beach with a shoreline of coconut palms, surrounded by a blue lagoon. Years later I found the island of my dreams, and it was my home since the 1970s (until I retired and moved to California). Most days were what I called 80/80 days: 80 degrees Fahrenheit and 80% humidity. It sometimes got down to 70 degrees in winter but not often. It could get up to 85 degrees and 95% humidity, but not often. The pace was unhurried, relaxed. The beauty was overwhelming, which is why I hardly ever left. Tropical fruits ripened and fell to the ground. Very little clothing was necessary. The good aspects of tropical life were obvious. What was not so obvious were the health issues that were beneath the surface. Yes, everything grew well and easily, so there was plenty to eat; but parasites, bacteria, fungi, mold, and toxins also proliferated. Staying healthy in the tropics was a full-time job. The environment had so many contagious pathogens in it that we had to be on guard all of the time. Water, food, people, pets, etc. passed things around. There were diseases I had never heard of like dengue, malaria, Ross River virus, Barmah Forest fever, onchocerca volvulus, Q-fever. For self-defense, I learned how to test for pathogens by Zincrometer. After many years of testing myself, family and friends, I moved on to business, testing local Polynesians, and then tourists.

At one point (when I first wrote this book and had it published as a Kindle eBook), I had helped more than 2,000 people to overcome cancer, diabetes, AIDS, arthritis—almost any disease you could think of. I used naturopathic protocols of Hulda Clark. I did a lot of research on new discoveries by internet and subscribed to many periodicals and journals. I incorporated traditional medicine from the Maori Polynesian pharmacopeia and massage. I worked with several Taunga (local Maori practitioners who pass traditional techniques down through their families from mother to daughter.) I became an expert Zincrometer tester, and people sent me saliva samples from all over the world. I tested the saliva on Zincrometer for pathogens; I then wrote and sent a report to each patient advising what they had and how to get rid of it. Most of my patients I never saw in person.

I volunteered at the local prison, where I had been able to prove beyond any doubt some revolutionary theories about the actual causes of mental illness: parasites in the brain are the cause of most mental disorders.

My personal health had been deteriorating for many years; and by the time I had reached my mid-fifties, my hands were so crippled with arthritis that I took early retirement from the motion-picture industry. Then I contracted dengue fever, a tropical disease spreading worldwide. While trying to recover from the dengue, I came down with fish poisoning, ciguatera, metagonimus yokogawa, and clonorchis sinensis. I had never been so ill in my life. The local doctors warned I would die the following day if my platelet count fell further. They had nothing to offer but pain-killing tablets; they had no cure for anything I was suffering with. I had been communicating with members of my family who are mostly Western medical practitioners, and they were sending all sorts of advice to me in the tropics.

My brother sent me an early version of a Hulda Clark zapper and her first book. It saved my life. I recovered and started studying Clark protocols. My nickname as a boy was "professor," as I have always been studious and a natural scientist. I used my research on myself first; and I completely cured many problems including my rheumatoid arthritis, poor vision, meningitis, and more. At this point I got in the best shape that I had been in years. Many friends and family had the same experience. My passion increased the more I learned. I realized that MDs were failing the world, mostly because of the pharmaceutical companies' influence over the medical profession, and their profit motivation. Historically, it all goes back hundreds of years to England's drug-pushing industries: Tobacco from American Indians, English black tea from China, Opium from Afghanistan, etc. England's entire economy had revolved around drug pushing all over the world, and today most big drug companies are still headquartered in London.

Law, which came to the world through the Old Testament of the Bible, was pushed by England along with the drugs. Today our world legal system is also dominated by big pharm, and medicine and law are hopelessly intertwined. The only way that the health of the world population can be bettered is if the world turns away from what and who is killing us. Regulation of the drug industry is of paramount importance. We will always need surgeons; but apart from surgery, medical doctors have no beneficial training to deal with lifestyle diseases. Lifestyle diseases are not only what are killing us but also diminishing the quality of our lives. MDs cannot diagnose or treat lifestyle disease. Instead they give drugs to alleviate symptoms and do not bother to discover the cause of illness. Millions of over-drugged zombies are bumping into each other—alive, but not well—wherever the drug pushers are in control. These people are not productive and are pulling everyone else down, along with world economies. We cannot afford to carry on like this. We must find the cause of an illness and remove it. Masking the symptoms with drugs to alleviate instead of cure disease shortens life and interferes with the enjoyment of life.

A prime example is streptococcus pneumonia. Because of the overuse of antibiotics, resistant strains of pneumonia have evolved that cannot be killed by antibiotics. The leading cause of death (when I first wrote this book) for people over 60 was pneumonia. (Today, the leading cause of death in the elderly is heart disease; for people in the 55 – 65 age group, it is cancer.) If a person with pneumonia saw an MD for the problem, the MD would have nothing to give the patient that worked. The overuse of antibiotics caused strains of streptococcus bacteria to evolve that antibiotics could not kill. Because pneumonia is a component of cancer, MDs cannot cure cancer effectively, either. Cancer cannot be stopped without killing strep pneumonia first. With only drugs and radiation for tools, the medical profession was deteriorating rapidly.

Governments are also influenced negatively in this scenario because big pharm has successfully lobbied governments worldwide to accept only their opinions instead of traditional medicine, or new discoveries. Insurance against illness for the most part covers only what a medical doctor or certified hospital deems to be good for the patient. The second leading cause of death worldwide is medical malpractice.

Staying alive and well on this planet requires taking complete responsibility for our own health. We must listen to what our bodies are telling us. The internet is available for almost everyone to use; and we can use it for diagnosis, cure, prevention, and longevity. Just look it up!

CANCER

Hulda Clark dealt with cancer almost exclusively the last few years of her life, along with AIDS, which is just cancer of the thymus. When I started my practice, I was a little reticent to deal with cancer because it has been hyped ridiculously by MDs as the scourge of life. After I had worked on a few patients with cancer, I realized it was just a lifestyle disease, and very curable, as long as people stay away from oncologists with their bogus treatments revolving around the misuse of radiation. Since radiation causes cancer (and death), the first step in ridding cancer is to stay away from cancer specialists' treatment. I have helped hundreds of people cure cancer of all types by simply removing the pathogens that caused the cancer. Radiation is a top pathogen for causing cancer, and radiation contamination is spreading worldwide as nuclear accidents continue and more fish is farmed. All farmed fish will carry radiation. Someday radiology will be an old-joke treatment like prefrontal lobotomy. When we look at what causes the disease we can understand, treat, and cure the disease. Cancer is basically an oxygen-deprivation malady. Our food processing removes oxygen so that the processed food can sit on the shelf for years without spoiling. This is great for the manufacturer and distributor, but it is terrible for the consumer. Consumer protection agencies worldwide are subverted by the pharmaceutical and other big business interests. The best way to avoid cancer is to avoid processed food. Fresh vegetables, fruit, and fish do not cause cancer. The best food to eat is what grows near or at home: vegetables home grown from your garden, fruit picked from your trees, and fish caught from the sea. Exercise can help as it increases oxygen supply. Only cold-pressed natural oils should be consumed (oxygenated): olive oil, flax seed oil, and coconut oil.

Turmeric, curry, cumin, Comino, and renga are some of the many names for a root that has been used in all societies worldwide since prehistory to prevent and cure cancer in humans. It is an annual root that grows everywhere, and once planted continues to produce year after year. In the Cook Islands (where I used to live), every home had a renga patch near the kitchen.

Curry powder is 60% turmeric and 40% cayenne pepper. Cancer is not as prevalent in countries like India (where turmeric is widely used) as it is in "developed" countries in North America and Europe, where food processing is king and the company is more important than the individual. Turmeric cannot be copyrighted as a cure as it is a common root growing everywhere, so you will not see drug companies pushing it.

Cleanses are critical to remove toxicity; body filters retain toxins and heavy metals that they remove from the body. These must be flushed out. Heavy metals open the door for other pathogens to enter the body. Liver and kidney cleanses are recommended. Four liters of water daily for 30 days with no other liquids consumed is one of the easiest and most effective ways to jump start kidneys, for example. Hulda Clark has many cleanse recipes in her books. European naturopath Alan Baklayan recommends chlorella tablets. I used to tell Polynesian people in the islands to go out on the reef and gather fresh seaweed to eat with meals. Japanese have made seaweed wrapped sushi popular. Vitamin D from the sun is essential.

Use frequency generation to the body of frequencies identified to kill the pathogens, which have been identified and located with Zincrometer testing. With Zincrometer location of fasciolopsis buski, a parasite which lives wherever flesh is dying from cancer, the affected organs are identified; and we can see how widespread the cancer is to estimate a timetable for cure.

Our bodies find parasites and encapsulate them, creating cysts that eventually become tumors, which then become malignant. So we must remove these tumors as we cure the cancer. I use Papain enzymes from the seeds and skin of papaya (pawpaw, nita, etc.). Papain shrinks tumors away. If you take the fresh fruit and cut away any green skin (phloridzin), place the rest of fruit, skin, seeds, flesh, and all, in a blender with one peeled banana or other fresh fruit to vary taste, blend, and consume a six-ounce glass daily, tumors shrink away rapidly. I also recommend graviola fruit, seeds, leaves, or tablets made from this tree for tumor shrinkage and parasite killing. Vitamin D is critical for avoidance of cancer as well as prevention: 20 minutes a day in direct sunlight to absorb the vitamin D, and of course the vitamin A must be adequate in body for the utilization of D.

All yellow to orange fruits and vegetables contain vitamin A; eat daily. Statistically, people who spend 20 minutes a day in the sun have a 70% less likelihood of contracting cancer. If a cancer patient has tested positive for radiation and/or fluazinam, sunlight is the best way to remove these pathogens. Avoid cancer allergens: chlorogenic acid, phloridzin, gallic acid, asbestos, chlorine, Lilly family (garlic, onion, etc.), mustard, all farmed shrimp and farmed fish, preserved meats, polyunsaturated oils, especially margarines, and isopropyl alcohol. If cancer is in the breast, skin, or brain, avoid all sweeteners. If cancer is in the colon or prostate, avoid using vinegar. Prostate and breast cancer can be cured by simply consuming pomegranate juice daily. Cancer pain is always caused by streptococcus bacteria. All cancer patients will test positive for Strep pneumonia, and it must be eliminated to cure cancer.

If one is tested positive for malaria and/or onchocerca volvulus or cytomegalovirus in the central nervous system, it is advanced cancer. If positive for hepatitis and sv-40, the sv-40 must be killed before working on the hepatitis. I have helped hundreds cure cancer and have never lost a previously untreated patient to cancer to date; but if I start on them after they have been abused by radiation from oncology, they sometimes die before I can remove the radiation. Statistically, 97% of cancer patients who have undergone chemotherapy die within five years of the first treatment. Patients who choose no treatment live much longer than patients who decide on chemotherapy and surgery.

There is a growing body of evidence that compounds in cannabis may shrink or slow the growth of tumors.

CANCER PROTOCOL

Test for fasciolopsis buski; if it is present, either cancer or pre-cancer is present in body. Test for OPT; if positive, cancer is active. Isopropyl alcohol positive is another indicator. Clostridium bacteria present if cancer is in thyroid; kill it as it produces isopropyl alcohol. Polonium is the other element present representing radiation. Aflatoxin and other mycotoxins and the mold that carries them must be removed to stop tumor growth and shrink tumors. Usually after the first day of treatment with varizapper, patients will test negative for cancer as it has been stopped; they will be negative for OPT (ortho phosphor tyrosine), and negative for isopropyl alcohol. Always test for OPT and isopropyl before and after each treatment with Zincrometer.

1. Cells become cancerous due to oxygen deficiency as the buski use up the oxygen. Exercise can help as it increases oxygen supply. Only cold-pressed natural oils should be consumed (oxygenated). Coconut oil, flax seed oil, olive oil. Organic raw sunflower, sesame, pumpkin, peanut in shell, almonds, walnuts, cashews, chestnut, etc. Seeds

and nuts should be eaten frequently after testing for and killing any mold on them or parasites in them.

2. Bromelain insures better delivery of oxygen to the cells through the blood, stops tumor growth, and inhibits spread of cancer. Take 2 tablets 3 times a day on an empty stomach.
3. Dental clean up, if mercury positive. Cancerous cells attract heavy metals which deplete the body of B-vitamins, so a B-complex should be taken or niacin amide. All heavy metals must be identified and removed.
4. Turmeric (renga) induces apoptosis (suicide) in cancer cells; use daily in cooking and grated raw on salads. Ginger and parsley help too.
5. Liver and kidney cleanse.
6. Biowave frequency generation with varizapper using Cancer driver for 21 days, then once or twice/week for maintenance. If tumor present, use tumor driver daily until tumor disappears, and take 200mcg of selenium daily. Oncovirus and tumor drivers speed the process.
7. Vegetarian diet best until all trace of cancer is gone. Papain (from pawpaw), an enzyme in the seeds and skin, produces tumor necrosis (shrinkage). One whole

pawpaw, remove any green parts and eat the remainder: seeds, skin, and all.

8. Avoid eating anything that has been in a microwave oven!
9. Use no hair dyes (unless they test well on zincrometer), or pain medications, as these cause and exacerbate cancer.
10. Vitamin D reduces cancer 50%! Spend 30 minutes every day in the sun to absorb vitamin D, and make sure you have adequate vitamin A in order to utilize the vitamin D. Vitamin D removes radiation.
11. Avoid cancer allergens: chlorogenic acid, phloridzin, and gallic acid, all Lilly family (onion, garlic), mustard, shrimp and shell fish, carrots. Eat no food containing phloridzin, no green (unripe) fruits, and no preserved meats: ham, corned beef, bacon, etc., no poly-unsaturated oils or margarines. Any member of cabbage family must be thoroughly cooked. Only roasted or boiled peeled potatoes—no russet potatoes, no fried. No watermelon, no maple syrup, no grains which have gallic acid preservative; no unpeeled apples, corn chips, whole wheat crackers, heavy cream or ice cream, raw eggs,

granola bars, margarine, potato chips, soy milk, low-fat yogurt. Consume as little coffee and black tea as possible.

12. Remove all unnatural chemicals from your mouth, diet, body, and home. Remove everything in your house that contains isopropyl alcohol. Read all ingredient labels to find them. Rubbing alcohol, most cosmetics, cold cereals, shampoo, toothpaste, etc.
13. If cancer is in the breast, skin, or brain, avoid sugar, honey, and all sweeteners. Check for aluminum build-up as this triggers breast cancer.
14. If cancer is in the colon or prostate, avoid using vinegar.
15. Black walnut, wormwood, and cloves are herbs to use for advanced cancer or large parasites which are hard to kill if in brain or bile duct; Clarks FX tincture drops, 10 drops 3 times daily for 4 days; retest to be sure large parasites killed. Available from www.drclark.com
16. Test drinking water for asbestos (in tap water on Rarotonga, in Fiji and New Zealand), chlorine, and polonium (radiation from water filters). Most tap water will test positive for mold and fungi which can be removed with common fungi driver step 1 and 2.

17. Prostate and breast cancer can be cured with pomegranate juice (remuna); one 8-oz glass/day. COQ10 reverses breast cancer and cures rapidly. Staph aureus bacteria is present in all breast cancer which comes from tooth infection; fix tooth infection, then kill staph, then remove gold and nickel.
18. According to the Journal of National Cancer Institute May 17, 2011, coffee prevents prostate cancer, 2 or more cups/day.
19. Cancer pain is always caused by streptococcus pneumonia. Look for with zincrometer and use pneumonia driver with zapper; oporo chili (cayenne pepper) kills strep bacteria—eat daily. Bromelain, gingko, cloves, and ginger, help the body to overcome.
20. Malaria connection: In advanced cancer test for malaria (plasmodium) and onchocerca parasites; if benzene is positive as well, use Tropical driver in conjunction with cancer and Oncovirus drivers. If cancer does not come negative right away, or returns positive in days, look for cytomegalovirus in the central nervous system and run onco through step 6. Onchocerca a factor in varicosity as

well so check for varicose veins and vision problems as in far sighted. Patient must take magnesium to counteract.

21. Positive for phosphate build up? Rhomanga or Percy's powders are best, or take alkaline salts to rebalance minerals. No red meats, potatoes, or tomatoes for a while or any vegetables from super phosphate fertilized fields. Calcium, magnesium, and potassium must increase.
22. Custard apple, soursop, graviola; this fruit was researched extensively as a cancer-curing fruit with 10,000 times the efficacy of chemo therapy for all cancer. One 6-oz glass of juice with 50% fruit and 50% water added daily. Crushed seeds kill parasites; tea from leaves is therapeutic. Seven leaves placed between pillow and case aids sleep.
23. Prostate cancer: Men will always test positive for cryptosporidium in their prostate as well as fasciolopsis buski. Evidence points to cryptosporidium as the cause of all prostate cancer; I also suspect another protozoan parasite giardia lamblia. I continue to research this theory, and others should as well, in order to reduce this pathogen in our food supply to stop prostate cancer. I

find cryptosporidium in processed junk food and Giardia lamblia in untreated water.

24. Hepatitis must be checked and removed with C.V. step 12 after sv-40 removed
25. I recommend Rhomanga tablets or Percy's powder to all patients with advanced cancer.
26. If cancer does not stop with treatment, test for mycobacterium tuberculosis and leprosy. Anyone who is positive for TB will also be positive for leprosy.
27. This sets up a holding pattern in body. C. parasite step 2+3 to kill TB followed by Tropical driver step 5 for leprosy. After this the regular cancer treatment will work.

LIVER CLEANSE PROCEDURE

Ingredients:

- Epsom salts, 4 level tablespoons, or 60 capsules from www.drclark.com
- Light Olive oil, half a cup
- Grapefruit juice, fresh; ¾ cup.
- L-tryptophan capsules, 1 to enable sleep if person is a light sleeper.
- Glass jar with lid.

Choose a day like a Saturday for the cleanse so that you will be able to rest the day after.

Take no pharmaceuticals that you can do without.

Eat a no-fat breakfast and lunch (no dairy). Fruit and vegetables seasoned with salt only are best.

2:00 pm: Do not eat or drink after 2 pm. If using Epsom salt powder, mix 4 level tablespoons of Epsom salts into 3 cups of water in a glass jar. Put the jar in the fridge to get ice cold.

6:00 pm: Drink one ¾ cup serving of the cold Epsom salt and water mixture, or take 15 Epsom salt capsules with ¾ cup of water.

8:00 pm; Drink another ¾ cup of Epsom salt mixture, or another 15 capsules with ¾ cup water.

9:45 pm: Mix ½ cup of the light olive oil and ¾ cup of grapefruit juice in your other jar and shake vigorously to combine

10:00 pm: Drink the oil and grapefruit potion with 1 tryptophan tablet if needed. Consume the entire contents within 5 minutes.

Lie down immediately on your back perfectly still for 20 minutes; go to sleep.

Next morning: Upon awakening take your third dose of Epsom salts (not before 6 am). Expect loose bowels. After movement, use flashlight to examine contents of toilet bowl. You should see tan or green pieces floating, which are the gallstones you have passed, along with movement, which should sink.

Two hours later take last dose of Epsom salts.

After 2 more hours, you may eat. Start with fruit juice; ½ hour later eat fruit. One hour later you may eat regular food. By dinner time you should feel recovered.

This cleanse is mostly Hulda Clark, but it is modified for my region. Use what is available where you live.

AIDS

Most diseases have more than one component. AIDS has many components, but three that make a person AIDS positive and active.

- Cytomegalovirus (sv-40)
- Benzene (coal oil)
- Fasciolopsis buski (parasite)

Streptococcus pneumonia is always present as well, and herpes carrying several STDs. If active for any length of time, the body will be accumulating parasites, bacteria, fungi, toxins, etc.

If Paragonimus westermani is present, benzene will be manufactured by this parasite. Zearalenone in the body increases paragonimus's ability to produce benzene. This is the pathogen which causes brain deterioration in HIV+ patients. We should try to discover the source of this contamination or the person may re-infect and get the AIDS back again. I find it mostly in tubers; check potatoes, beets, carrots, and onions for this parasite. It is almost always found in old carrots. It is often in untreated water. If a person dies from AIDS, it will be because of paragonimus in the brain as it causes faulty decisions and inability to follow prevention and cure programs.

Eurytrema pancreaticum is usually positive as this is the parasite that invites SV-40 to the body. Cytomegalovirus lives in the thymus, of course, but it also hides in the central nervous system. If malaria and/or dengue fever positive, the cytomegalovirus will hold malaria and dengue in the CNS and cause night sweats and encephalitis, sometimes for years. Once the sv-40 is negative in the CNS, the malaria and dengue can be easily cured.

Nerve parasites (herpetic disease) are usually present in all aids patients; test for echinoporphyrium and echinostoma as these welcome other pathogens into body. Hepatitis is usually present and will not come out until sv-40 is negative.

If a person has one or two of the components, the cure is simple, fast, and easy. Once the three main components are all present, the disease is active and spreading. The longer the disease is in the body, the harder it is to get rid of; but I have never found anyone whom I could not completely cure of AIDS. A few years ago a young couple with a newborn baby tested positive for AIDS. The baby was cured in less than an hour. The mother tested negative in three days. The father took three weeks, mainly because he had it longest, and also because he would not do cleanses as advised.

I have worked with people who were diagnosed with AIDS positive 20 or more years ago; some were in complete remission, some were still positive even though both had been on the pharm cocktail. The only difference I could discern was that the ones who had changed their lifestyle had cured themselves, testing negative for all components. Those who had not made the lifestyle changes were positive for all components, and they still had AIDS in spite of taking the pharm cocktail for many years.

AIDS being a type of cancer, the cure of AIDS is similar to curing any other cancer. Kill the pneumonia, kill the virus, remove the benzene, and kill the fasciolopsis buski. When the patient is negative for cancer, he will be negative for AIDS. This is another hyped disease by big pharm that they claim is not curable, so you must buy their drugs to "control" the incurable disease. What complete nonsense. There is an incredible amount of disinformation out there about AIDS; most of this confusion of course helps big pharm to sell and profit. Scare people and they will cough up their cash. It's reminiscent of Joseph Goebbels, Adolph Hitler's press officer, who said that if you tell a lie often enough eventually people will believe it. The spread of AIDS, for example, is not necessarily from intercourse with an infected person. Cytomegalovirus is in the environment. It is in the water supply of many countries. If one person in a household has AIDS, he can spread it to others sharing the accommodation through hand towels. Why does Africa have more AIDS than other continents? Because Africa is awash in benzene (coal oil), which is the triggering component that activates the disease. Why is it more common in people who indulge in anal intercourse? Because the anus has no natural lubrication, and the lubricants that big pharm provides contain benzene. This is why many homosexuals claim that the pharmaceutical industry is targeting them.

Fear of AIDS is as ridiculous as fear of swine flu, which was just a common flu hyped by big pharm as deadly. Syphilis and herpes are far more difficult to eradicate than AIDS. I have seen AIDS in the wealthy and the poor, children and adults, homosexual and heterosexual. Many test positive for the virus as they have picked it up from their environment. As long as they avoid exposure to benzene and do not attract fasciolopsis, it will be dormant. Millions were exposed to the virus by polio vaccine in the 1960s and 70s when cells from the rhesus monkey were used to develop the vaccine (which has never been proven to have worked then or now). Again, this was big pharm at work spreading disease for profit. A personal friend and very good MD, who specialized in AIDS research and devoted his entire practice to it for ten years, realized what nonsense was being sold as truth and returned to general practice. I get queries from all over the world, and I am constantly amazed at what people believe to be true with absolutely no proof from MDs.

Most AIDS patients will be positive for herpetic disease, which is what has welcomed the many pathogens into the body. Echinoporphyrium and echinostoma are likely to be zincrometer positive but hard to find; look in sublingual and parotid glands, central nervous system, and of course, muscle tissue and lungs.

On June 11, 2011, male tested positive for fasciolopsis buski, SV-40, strep pneumonia, OPT, isopropyl alcohol, eurytrema pancreaticum, and staphylococcus aureus, all in the thymus (blood filter). But no benzene; he had not contracted Paragonimus, which produces benzene: So he was negative for AIDS. He had all of the components except benzene, so he had cancer of the thymus, but not AIDS yet. We were able to kill all of the pathogens and he did not contract AIDS. This was an older man who had not had intercourse for many years and was a regular returning patient who had not been positive for any of the pathogens previously. He had acquired all of the pathogens from his environment!

Suffice it to say, AIDS is curable; it is cancer of the blood filter, and it is not a death sentence.

HIV/AIDS PROTOCOL

1. Test by zincrometer for buski and sv-40 in the Thymus gland, OPT, isopropyl alcohol; if present HIV positive. Herpes with candida and chlamydia is always present; cure this as it will suppress immune system. Test for hepatitis; usually there. Check for shigella flexemi in the thymus as well.
2. If benzene is also present in body, then AIDS can develop. Test for malaria, and if positive, use tropical disease driver in conjunction with Oncovirus and AIDS drivers. Malaria positives should avoid honey, aspirin, and lemons. No gold in mouth or on body. Avoid French fries and potato chips.
3. Liver cleanse to get rid of the benzene after the Paragonimus has been eradicated and zearalenone has been killed. High doses of detox vitamins and supplements such as A, E, C, selenium, niacin amide, ginseng. Zappication.
4. Biowave frequency generation using Oncovirus driver and HIV driver daily. Testing with zincrometer weekly until all trace of benzene and buski is gone. Continue to

zap once every 3 or 4 days for a couple of months to make sure patient does not re-infect from environment.

5. Check partners and family.
6. Black walnut hulls, wormwood, cloves: In FX tincture available from www.drclark.com FX tincture: 10 drops under tongue 3 times per day for 4 days; then 4 drops per week for one year.
7. HIV positive patients are susceptible to molds, ergot, sterigmatocystin, and zearalenone. They should avoid whole grains and take 1500mg niacin amide/day to counteract. Common fungi driver to kill.
8. Diet should avoid any food product that says diet, fat free, salt free, decaffeinated, defatted, lite, polyunsaturated, or imitation as these foods are denatured. Avoid cooking foods over charcoal as this produces benzo pyrenes.
9. Halt illicit drug use as in cocaine, methamphetamine, and check labels of all products used for benzene, naphthalene, aniline, phenol, hydroquinone, Xylene, toluene. No soft drinks containing benzoic acid for preservation.

10. Use renga (turmeric) daily. Take fresh root and grate on to salads and into cooked foods.
11. Suspect foods that may contain gallic acid which is the trigger for SV40 (simian virus) release. Peel apples before eating. Avoid corn chips, whole wheat crackers, heavy whipping cream, raw eggs, granola bars, margarine, polyunsaturated oils, canned black olives, shelled peanuts, potato chips, soy beverages, soy lecithin, and low fat yogurt.
12. AIDS is a type of cancer; refer to cancer Protocol for further advice.
13. Make sure that the water you are drinking and cooking with is pure and free of pathogens. Mold must be eliminated if present from Zincrometer analysis; common fungi driver, usually step 1 and 2 but retest to make sure no mold present as it carries whatever pathogens are in the water.
14. Thioctic acid 3/day for 2 weeks for metal removal.
15. Test for and kill echinoporphyrium and echinostoma parasites with ALS driver steps 10+11. See protocol.

16. Discover where the pathogens came from in the environment so patient can learn to avoid them and not get the disease back.

DIABETES

The word diabetes comes from Greek. It means excessive urine. Doctors have added high glucose levels in blood and extreme thirst symptoms. According to Hulda Clark, diabetes is another lifestyle disease. It has absolutely no connection to genetics, but MDs keep telling people that it does. They say if your parents had it you will have it, as you are disposed to acquiring diabetes. That is complete nonsense. If your parents had poor eating habits, and they teach their children to eat the same processed food they do, then of course the children can acquire the same malady. If the children are intelligent enough to see that they should change the way they eat and live, they will never get the disease their parents had. Diabetes is easily cured if people make the changes in lifestyle. It is caused by faulty diet and pathogens in the pancreas. Zincrometer analysis of pancreas to find the parasite; usually eurytrema pancreaticum, but it can be others. Look for echinoporphyrium in pancreas, which cause the pancreas to enlarge from the cysts the body creates to protect from the parasite. The food trigger is high fructose corn syrup. The environmental triggers are methanol and phloridzin. Radiation or bacterial infection in pancreas are the usual causes of what MDs call type one diabetes, which of course is not diabetes at all; but it is an inflamed pancreas that stops generating insulin.

In most developed countries manufacturers are required to label product ingredients that are known pathogens. High fructose corn syrup is a well-known pathogen that is the cause of amputation in diabetics. It is a cheap sweetener so very attractive to unscrupulous manufacturers, and people who cannot afford products sweetened with cane sugar. High fructose corn syrup causes varicosity, and varicose veins are veins that come close to the skin instead of in the flesh where they are supposed to be. Poor circulation of blood with little oxygen in it leads to death of tissue, usually starting in extremities. First the toes are amputated and then farther up the legs they go. Removal of high fructose corn sweetener from the diet is essential to avoid amputation. The most common sources are soft drinks and canned fruit, but it is very common in any foods and beverages that need sweetening, even some beers.

Methanol (wood alcohol) removal is also essential, as methanol is a chemical which triggers eurytrema pancreaticum parasite to produce diabetic symptoms. Liver cleansing will remove methanol from body filters, as will chlorella (seaweed), and Zappication will neutralize. It must be removed from the environment to avoid recontamination. This is the hard part because so many manufacturers add methanol to their products, as it is a lubricant. Mostly it is the big companies who do this. Read labels to avoid it, but not all manufacturers list methanol, even though their products test positive for it. This makes for good practice on your Zincrometer; test everything you put in or on yourself.

Avoid foods containing phloridzin; this is a chemical that occurs in fruits and vegetables as a preservative, which allows food to ripen slowly: never eat green fruit! Peel the green skin off of potatoes, tomatoes, apples, etc. Raw foods are best; reduce consumption of cooked foods. Grapefruit or its juice lowers glucose and insulin levels while burning fat. A high intake of dairy products increases insulin resistance. Eggs and mayonnaise should be avoided for a while to avoid salmonella and ergot.

Exercise is very important—just 30 minutes a day. You don't need to participate in iron-man athletics. Walking or swimming does the job. When I get really large overweight diabetics, I start them just sitting in a pool or ocean beach and waving their arms and legs back and forth in the water to lose weight and slowly get their strength back so that they can walk, etc.

Check if positive for asbestos; it accumulates in weak organs. Eliminate it from your environment.

Graviola is a tree from the Amazon rain forest which grows easily in any sub-tropical to tropical setting. The seeds from the fruit kill the parasites in the pancreas. Seeds, fruits, leaves—everything from this tree is beneficial. It is available in tablet form from www.rain-tree.com.

If you are taking diuretics, stop immediately as diuretics cause and exacerbate diabetes. Ignorant MDs still prescribe diuretics to diabetics.

Dissolve a half teaspoon of cinnamon in honey daily to reduce cholesterol; but if patients are positive for echinoporphyrium, they must avoid cinnamon until echinoporphyrium is negative. To reduce glucose levels dramatically, use ¼ teaspoon of powdered cloves daily.

If purpura is present, avoid all corn products. Phoma lingam fungi causes "black leg disease" increasing possibility of an amputation from gangrene. Common fungi driver kills phoma lingam.

People who are positive for Alzheimer's and diabetes must conquer the diabetes because insulin causes the brain to form plaques which can exacerbate the Alzheimer's.

Radiation should be checked for in all patients; but when I am told that the patient was diagnosed type-one diabetic, I check radiation immediately as diabetes is often misdiagnosed when radiation is in the pancreas: similar symptoms but not diabetes. This is usually from eating farmed fish contamination or taking fish oil capsules.

MRSA bacteria in the pancreas will cause infection and stop insulin production; common bacteria driver step 11+12 and the pancreas will start insulin again! No more type 1 diabetes.

DIABETES PROTOCOL

1. Test for pancreas and kidney infestation of parasites eurytrema pancreaticum, sheep liver fluke, echinoporphyrium recurvatum, and radiation. Triggers are methanol and phloridzin. NOT SUGAR!!
2. Biowave generation using Diabetes driver daily for 2 weeks; then once weekly for maintenance.
3. Methanol removal is critical; liver cleanse will do this, but no products containing methanol should be used; see tested safe products list or test on your Zincrometer.
4. Niacin amide 500 mg. every 6 hours = 1500 mg/day to reduce toxicity.
5. L-Tryptophan reduces hunger for carbohydrates and lowers blood sugar levels; take one capsule daily after evening meal.
6. Prescribe flax seed oil, selenium, bromelain and/or pycnogenol, to avoid amputations. G-5 poultice relieves quickly.
7. Exercise daily for 30 minutes.
8. Avoid any foods containing phloridzin, all green (unripe) fruits, all pork, corned beef, all poly-unsaturated oil

products, especially margarines. Anything from cabbage family must be thoroughly cooked (cauliflower, kohlrabi, squash, Brussels sprouts, broccoli, etc.). Cashew nuts. Millet. Chicken and eggs. After 5 days on this diet, the diabetic symptoms will disappear.

9. Diabetics must avoid high fructose corn syrup; consume absolutely no soft drinks or canned fruits containing corn syrup.
10. Recommend the liver cleanse.
11. Dental clean up and especially remove any gold from mouth and wear no gold jewelry.
12. All sources of methanol must be removed from environment.
13. Diet should consist of mainly raw foods (full of enzymes); avoid cooked foods as much as possible.
14. Fresh grapefruit or its juice lowers glucose and insulin levels while burning fat.
15. Avoid high intake of dairy products as this dramatically increases insulin resistance. Check for and remove salmonella or go on a no egg or mayonnaise diet.
16. Graviola (soursop, kataraapa, and custard apple) crushed seeds kill eurytrema parasite; tea from leaves and fruit

eaten or juiced very beneficial. Graviola Max Tablets available at www.rain-tree.com.

17. If you are taking diuretics stop as they cause diabetes.
18. Half a teaspoon of cinnamon with 1 teaspoon honey daily reduces harmful cholesterol levels. But if the diabetic is positive for echinoporphyrium; avoid cinnamon until echino negative.
19. One-fourth a teaspoon of cloves daily reduces glucose levels dramatically.
20. If purpura present avoid corn products.
21. Go to www.healingmatters.com and click on fats and oils for more info; cook only with butter, coconut oil, or olive oil at low temperatures.
22. Zincrometer test for phoma lingam and kill with c. fungi driver as it causes black leg (amputation).
23. Check for MRSA in pancreas; strep and staph infection. C. bacteria steps 11+12.
24. Indicative symptoms: Excessive urination, hunger, and thirst.

PRODUCTS FULL OF DANGEROUS CHEMICALS

Once proficient in Zincrometer testing, we should test all products ingested or that we apply to the skin. Do not believe what is on the labels about ingredients; they lie! Place product on left plate of Zincrometer. Place pathogens to test for on right plate. Hold probe in lower right hand with pinky and ring finger holding in place. Pencil probe in upper right hand with thumb and index and middle finger holding, (as you would hold a pen). Apply point to left index finger at first joint, listening for resonance or flat sound emanating from Zincrometer. This is great practice for experience.

Legal constraints prevent me from publishing the names of companies whose products are full of dangerous chemicals and pathogens, but the list would surprise you if I could. If a product is heavily advertised and widely promoted, it is suspect. These huge conglomerates have hundreds of lawyers working for them, ready to pounce on anyone who criticizes their employers. Greed corrupts the market place. Do not believe the lies. If you cannot test, avoid large companies' products.

Farmed fish, especially shrimp, frequently carry radiation, herbicides, fungicides, etc. Eat only wild caught fish and eat nothing from the bottom of the sea or lake.

Eggs can carry mycotoxins, especially patulin and ergot.

Tubers must be tested as they often carry parasites. Potatoes, beets, and carrots that are peeled thoroughly are less dangerous. In this small island state where I live many tubers are imported; russet potatoes from New Zealand are the source of Lyme disease here. I have tested russet potatoes in Australia and America that were also carrying ascaris and borrelia and bacteroides. Beets bring the echino nerve parasites. Oranges grown anywhere can carry echino as well. Bananas and papaya grown near septic systems pick up septic contamination. Tomatoes easily pick up and pass bacteria to the consumer. Carrots are fine if they are fresh with the green tops still on; once the green is removed you can't tell their age, and the older the carrot the more pathogens it will carry.

Anything grown in New Zealand is likely to be contaminated with asbestos and heavy metals as these pathogens are in the New Zealand water system.

ARTHRITIS

Arthritis is a very interesting disease. It has many types and many causes, so it is very difficult to diagnose and treat. First, test for and kill all parasites in the body; ancylostoma caninum is a common cause, especially of knee pain, as this parasite likes to live behind the knee cap. Faciola hepaticus, trichinella, strongyloides, and fasciolopsis buski are suspects. Toxicity is the next thing to look for. Thallium is the most toxic substance known to man. One drop ingested will kill a human being in minutes. Teflon coated pots and pans are the usual source of thallium poisoning. Never use these coated cooking appliances. I advise cast iron cookware as the best for cooking anything for many reasons; Hulda Clark preferred stainless steel.

Cleanses are essential to remove toxins. Another exacerbating toxin is alcohol; if arthritis sufferers are drinkers they must always eat something before drinking alcohol because alcohol on an empty stomach triggers a gout attack! Especially cold beer causes formation of oxalic crystals which attack joints that have been injured at some time. As beer gets older mycotoxins develop in it; make sure beer is fresh. Soft drinks preserved with benzoic acid can cause gout as benzene in kidneys causes multiple problems in the body. Read the ingredients of soft drinks; no high fructose corn syrup on benzoic acid. Nocardia asteroids (dental bacteria) can also trigger gout attacks. It is easily killed with frequency generator using tooth or sore throat drivers. Some rheumatoid arthritis is caused by vitamin B3 deficiency. Niacin amide tablets will correct this. Taking1500 mg/day will dissolve calcium deposits and the fingers and toes will straighten out again. If swelling is a problem, zinc tablets reduce inflammation; take one a day or eat seeds and nuts, which contain zinc. Edema can be exacerbated with patulin and ergot; remove with C. fungi driver.

Cholesterol build up is frequently a factor; ½ teaspoon of cinnamon daily reduces cholesterol and inflammation. Pomegranate fruit or juice reduces arthritic pain, blocks blood clots, and removes plaque from arteries and veins. Food allergies exacerbate arthritis in some people: sugar, wheat, citrus, pork, night shade family (tomato, potato, eggplant, green pepper), chicken and eggs, mayonnaise, cabbage family (cabbage, broccoli, cauliflower, Brussels sprouts contain cyanide), and peas. Acidity is sometimes an issue; increase alkalinity with magnesium; 300 mg tablet with milk just before bed. For chronic pain, test for and remove chromium. Streptococcus pneumonia is a pain bringer too, which is easily subdued with frequency generation. Check for phosphate build up if the patient is a smoker; tobacco adds phosphate to body. Mineral balance is critical. Psoriatric arthritis if positive for psoriasis and arthritis; itching around hairline and elbows usually precedes an attack. It is caused by zearalenone mycotoxins and exacerbated by acidic diet, stress, helicobacter bacteria, haemopholis, campylobacter, meningococcal bacteria, and nocardia asteroids, which are frequently in bread and tap water.

Viruses can cause arthritic symptoms; check for Lyme disease with Coxsackie virus, borrelia, and ascaris. Dengue fever is spreading rapidly all over the world, and the primary symptoms of dengue are stiff neck and aching joints (the English called it "break bone disease"). It causes arthritic symptoms, but it is a fever similar to a virus.

Entamoeba coli, which carries hepatitis D+ E, inflames connective tissue in the body and can be mistaken for arthritis! Tennis elbow is frequently just this; test for entamoeba and Hepatitis and locate in connective and or muscle tissue and kill it with tropical disease driver step 7 for parasite and step 10 for hepatitis.

Common fungi patulin, mainly from root crops, can infect sciatic nerve and cause lower back pain. Peel all tubers thoroughly before cooking. Lilly family, onion, garlic etc.; submerge in basin of water with a dash of vinegar for 15 minutes, or apply common fungi driver to kill mold.

Test for ergot or zap baked goods, eggs, and red wines with c. fungi driver step 9 for bursitis.

Identifying the type and cause of the arthritis can be difficult, but if we persist we can cure all arthritis in the body.

ARTHRITIS PROTOCOL

1. If fasciolopsis buski or faciola hepatica is present in body, use parasite driver and eat ginger, turmeric, and parsley in salads and use in cooking.
2. Cherries fresh or canned dissolve oxalic crystals; just 6 to 12/day for gout relief.
3. Flax seed or coconut oil daily on food or take 2 tablespoons/day. High in omega-3 fatty acid unlike polyunsaturated oils which are low in omega-3 and high in omega-6.
4. Toxicity problem: kidney cleanse and liver cleanse.
5. Avoid alcohol (especially beer), coffee, tea, and caffeinated beverages. After symptoms are relieved, wine may be consumed with food without return of symptoms. Never drink alcohol on an empty stomach. Always check *use-by dates*.
6. Biowave frequency generation with arthritis driver daily until symptoms are relieved. Gout attacks are frequently caused by dental bacteria; use tooth bacteria driver.
7. One-fourth teaspoon of cinnamon daily reduces cholesterol levels and inflammation.

8. Some rheumatoid arthritis is caused by vitamin B deficiency; Niacin amide tablets will correct this; 500 mg. 3 times/day = 1500 mg/day if there are calcium deposits.
9. Zincrometer test: place bone and bone marrow slides or testing vials on left plate; test for strongyloides (thread worm), hook worm, and trchinella; if positive zap frequencies for them with gel pads affixed to area of pain as they can get in to the bone itself and cause platelet problems.
10. If swollen, zinc tablets reduce inflammation; one a day. Pumpkin seeds. Bromelain/magnesium/niacinamide flush; 1000 mg bromelain/500 mg niacinamide/100 mg magnesium 3 times a day; morning mid-day and evening, all on empty stomach between meals.
11. Maori in NZ have eaten green lip mussels for many years to relieve arthritis. A new pharmaceutical, Lyprinol, is made from these mussels.
12. Pomegranate fruit and juice reduces arthritic pain, blocks blood clots and removes plaque from arteries.
13. Test for thallium; if positive it must be removed by cleansing and Zappication.

14. Food allergies that can exacerbate arthritis in some people: sugar, wheat, citrus, pork, night shade family (tomato, potato, eggplant, peppers) chicken, eggs, mayo, cabbage family, and peas.
15. If acidity is the problem, take alkaline salt 2 capsules every 4 hours until relieved or 300 mg magnesium capsule with a glass of milk before bed each night.
16. Chronic pain? Look for chromium and streptococcus pneumonia; if present use pneumonia driver and starve body of chromium, which feeds the strep. No metals, jewelry, teeth, etc. Also check for phosphates and remove with magnesium to counteract phosphates, especially if patient is a smoker, since tobacco adds phosphates to body. Check on biotest for too much phosphate and too little magnesium, calcium, and potassium.
17. Psoriatric arthritis: if patient tests positive for psoriasis and arthritis and has dry flaky patches of skin on scalp, elbows, and knees. Skin problems usually precede or are in conjunction with arthritis attack. Caused by acidic diet, stress, nocardia asteroides, helicobacter, haemopholis,

meningococcal or campylobacter; if positive remove as they are frequently in water, bread, and environment.

18. Test for fungi in all food as it exacerbates nerve problems with arthritis, especially sciatic nerve issues. If Zincrometer proficient, place slide or copy of sciatic nerve on left plate of Zincrometer, pathogens on right plate. See what is in sciatic nerve to know what must be killed. If bursa present relieve with common fungi driver step 9.
19. Check for virus which causes arthritic symptoms. Check for Lyme disease (Coxsackie virus, borrelia, ascaris, dengue, malaria, Ross River, Barmah Forest, anthrax (hoof and mouth disease, melioilitis, burkholderia, etc.).
20. Rice is frequently contaminated with human parasites when fertilized with human feces; it is a source for acquiring the parasites which bore into bones. Test all rice before cooking or eating. Hulda Clark stated that all brown rice carries pathogens White rice from Thailand tests well; rice from India and Viet Nam always has parasites, as they use human feces to fertilize. Best rice is white rice from Australia, Turkey, Mexico, or California.

21. Worm pets as they can carry the arthritis parasites to you.

RESPIRATORY DISEASES

As human beings the most important thing for good health is the ability to process oxygen. Back in the 1950s and 60s air quality became a very popular subject of discussion. Cities worldwide worked to remove "smog" from their air. A great deal of scientific investigation was focused on air—what it looked like and what was in it, etc. We know a lot now as a tremendous body of knowledge is the result of all the investigation over a 60-year period. Most cities have better visibility today in spite of the fact that populations, traffic, etc. have multiplied. Asthma is on the rise. Lyme disease is spreading. Processed food has had the oxygen removed from it more thoroughly, which benefits the vendor but kills the consumer.

I have personally suffered respiratory problems my entire life; my parents moved to California when I was ten years old, because an eye-ear-nose-and-throat specialist told them I would breathe better there. There was no improvement, of course, as the same pathogens are found worldwide. When I was drafted into the US army during the Viet Nam war, I was sent to Viet Nam and noticed that my breathing was the best it had ever been to that date. Probably the nine shots that I received prior to flight to Asia killed whatever parasites had been in my lungs since childhood. After discharge from service, I was right back to weak lungs again. Hulda Clark taught me what to look for, and I breathe very well now; thank you Hulda.

In the tropics the main parasite that inhabits people's lungs is ascaris, whereas in temperate climates it is enterobius vermicularis (pin worm). Fifty percent of tourists to the Cook Islands come from New Zealand, which has the highest rates of asthma in the world per population. When I Zincrometer test New Zealanders, they frequently harbor pin worm, so I kill it to get rid of their malady. In the island population I detected and killed the ascaris parasites, but I also looked for radiation, dengue fever, malaria, TB, salmonella, pneumonia, fungus, mold, and dirofilaria immitis (heart worm). If any of the above is present, dairy products will exacerbate the condition. I have never tested a single jar of mayonnaise from any manufacturer that did not test positive for salmonella on the zincrometer.

Pork products can cause respiratory problems for many people, especially Asians. Flax seed oil is the main supplement I advise to strengthen respiration. Omega fatty acids imbalance can be contributory as well. In fish oil omegas are in balance; but if a person eats beef, the omegas are out of balance with too much 5 and 6 and not enough 3. Fish is also the best way to get our protein; but we need to eat the skin as the oil is between the skin and flesh. I have never tested any fish oil supplement which did not test positive for metagonimus yokogawa, so I never recommend anyone take fish oil supplements. Flax seed oil, olive oil, and coconut oil all have omegas in balance. No margarine or polyunsaturated oil of any kind is any good for anything as it has had the oxygen removed from it.

Vitamin D deficiency is another factor. We must spend a minimum of 20 minutes a day in direct sunlight to get our vitamin D, and make sure you ingest an adequate supply of vitamin A since they work together. Yellow to orange fruits and vegetables contain vitamin A; consume daily.

When I first went to the tropics I was rather naive and believed what "authorities" had to say. I quickly learned that "authorities" are frequently wrong, and sometimes they just lie. Tuberculosis was a disease that the authorities said was conquered in the South Pacific and no longer an issue there. The first years of my practice I didn't test for it. Then I saw a report on TB and how it was on the rise in tropical areas of the world. Our public health authorities said they saw less than one new case per year. How could the Cook Islands be the only tropical country in the world that had no TB when every other country did? I started to test for it and was amazed. This was a learning experience for me in cancer treatment as well, because I could see that certain people who did not respond well to cancer treatment had TB. Once I had killed the TB the cancer was easy to cure. I started to check all patients for TB. Average per year of new TB patients I detected and completely cured = 100, about what all the rest of the countries average per population.

Leprosy is a side effect of TB, so anyone who tests positive for TB will also be positive for leprosy, and it should be removed as well. Leprosy cannot be cured until the TB has been eradicated. That's only ten minutes on the generator. If anyone has TB it creates a holding pattern in the body and it is hard to get rid of many pathogens until the TB has been dealt with. The type of TB that we saw mostly in the islands was aviary tuberculosis (from chickens), and it is a childhood disease usually contracted by pubescent children collecting eggs and handling chickens or drinking tap water that carries mycobacterium tuberculosis. Other respiratory problems are easy to deal with once the TB is gone. Use children's disease driver step 9 in varizapper. The 2013 TB epidemic across the South Pacific taught me a lot about TB as half of the patients I saw had tuberculosis and some families were passing it around like a hot potato. While testing food I found all of the components of an epidemic called Zika in potatoes which included Para tuberculosis; now I could tell how to avoid acquisition as well as cure it.

Mold and fungi with the mycotoxins they make add congestion to the body, and it is frequently in sinus and lungs; identify with zincrometer and remove with common fungi driver. Griseofulvin mycotoxin from mold carries TB and many pathogens. Cryptosporidium positive in lungs causes congestion and it is in most processed food. Common parasite driver step 6. Radiation build up in lungs is the most difficult type of congestion to eradicate as it requires removal of the radiation. Zappication and C. fungi step 2 help to neutralize; vitamin D from the sun and cleanses and chlorella over time will get rid of it.

ASTHMA, EMPHYSEMA, BRONCHITIS, RESPIRATORY AILMENTS PROTOCOL

1. Test for Ascaris, pin worm, dengue, malaria, TB, Salmonella, pneumonia, radiation, fungi, cryptosporidium, and dirofilaria immitis, griseofulvin, patulin, ergot, and asbestos.
2. Remove cow's milk and products from diet as they usually contain shigella bacteria.
3. If Salmonella is detected, remove eggs and mayonnaise from diet. When preparing eggs, crack the shell and deposit it on a flat saucer. Look at it. If the yolk is high and well rounded, the egg is fresh. If the yolk breaks or is flat, don't feed to your family; it will test positive for salmonella bacteria.
4. No pork or pork products should be eaten.
5. Liver cleanse indicated.
6. Asthma, bronchitis, throat, sinusitis, or allergy driver daily for two weeks depending on where the congestion is. Then twice per week for reinforcement.
7. Supplements: Flax seed oil daily. Pycnogenol or other ant-oxidant.

8. Asthma can be caused and exacerbated by imbalance in omega fat consumption: too much omega 6 and not enough omega 3. Use only cold pressed natural oils: flax seed oil, olive oil, and coconut oil. No margarine or polyunsaturated oils of any kind, no fried chicken, or farmed fish. Never take fish oil supplements.
9. Vitamin D deficiency causes asthmatic symptom; spend at least 20 minutes in sun daily to absorb vitamin D and make sure that you have adequate vitamin A in your body as A+D work together. Yellow to orange fruits and vegetables contain vitamin A; consume daily.
10. Zearalenone, ergot, and griseofulvin must be tested for and eliminated from all water, foods, and patients frequently; common fungi driver with varizapper.
11. Pin worm (enterobius vermicularis) is acquired from eating brown rice or Asian rice.
12. Asbestos causes mesothelioma which is deadly. Locate where the asbestos is in the body; it accumulates where the weakest organ of body is. Frequently this is in lungs as asbestos is in the environment and in processed food.

13. Russet potatoes should not be eaten unless they test negative for parasites ascaris and paragonimus, which is unlikely.

CAUSE OF MOST MENTAL DISORDERS

From headaches to schizophrenia, are they all caused by parasites?

I noticed in my practice that people who tested positive for one or more parasites in the brain had common denominators: depression, manic depression, inability to focus, psychopathic behavior, short-term memory loss, dizziness, headaches, poor eyesight, macular degeneration, etc. When I killed the parasites that I identified with zincrometer testing and located in the brain, I noticed, and the patients noticed, that behavior changed! Working with sick people daily left me exposed to many pathogens, which I sometimes acquired from them. When I felt my brain was not performing and tested positive for one or more parasites and located them in my brain, I also experienced the symptoms. I found it difficult to work if I had a brain parasite, as my ability to focus my thinking was affected. Because of my school years in psychology, this piqued my interest, and I started to study the phenomenon. My findings made me curious; the more I looked at it, the easier it was to draw corollaries and come to conclusions.

Naegleria fowleri has been identified by alternative health practitioners for many years as the cause of Alzheimer's when coupled with aluminum toxicity; that was a start. I proved this to myself with zincrometer identification of the parasite and location in the brain with aluminum. When I killed the parasite and removed the aluminum, the deterioration stopped immediately. When I prescribed gingko biloba, the grey cells regenerated and patients' memory improved, and their long-term prognosis of early death was thwarted. That was the beginning.

Toxoplasma gondii was the next parasite I looked at. UCLA research found this parasite to be a factor in automobile accidents, concluding that it affected a person's ability to make correct decisions in traffic. I found it mainly in teenagers and identified it as part of the reason for teen suicide (wrong decision obviously), and I suspect that this is also why teens are statistically more likely to have auto accidents. I had a patient whose mother was a school principal, who wanted to know why her daughter, a star pupil, had failed her exams. She tested positive for

Toxoplasma; I killed it and wrote a letter to her teachers explaining what she had and that they should please allow her to retest. She excelled after the parasites were no longer in her brain. I could give many more examples.

Paragonimus westermani: A close relative at the age of 16 tested positive for this, and it was located in the brain. Symptoms from this parasite are very similar to Toxoplasma gondii. This young man went from top student to failing student, and also made wrong decisions about with whom to associate; and he was having problems with school officials, security personnel, local police, and at home. He was in trouble on all fronts. After removal of the Paragonimus, his behavior normalized, his grades improved, and he exhibited no more antisocial behavior. To my thinking this is the most dangerous parasite that I know of, as it is the hardest to kill and it is in the environment in so many places and types of food.

Ascaris causes skin disease scabies, but if it is in the body laying thousands of eggs, it gets into the stomach, lungs, and eventually the brain. It resides in the short-term memory area of the brain, making us forgetful, especially of names, dates, and places. If we acquire Bacteroides fragilis, and/or borrelia borgdorferi and Chlamydia, we have Lyme disease. Lyme was originally thought to be a New England disease, from a deer living in the Appalachian Mountains, which carried ticks, and if the tick bit a human after the deer, Lyme would result. After Lyme epidemics in Europe, Asia, New Zealand, Australia, etc., most realized that the original research was faulty. In Lyme the ascaris parasite is always in the brain and causes massive problems with normal brain function. It is very difficult to kill, and the literature will tell you that people frequently suffer for up to two years with this disease. Once I have removed these pathogens the brain performs normally immediately.

Schistosoma haematobium, japonicum, and mansoni: These parasites can get as large as your finger in the brain. When that occurs it forces the brain against the side of the skull, causing migraine headaches, seizures, coma, and death.

This is well documented on the Internet.

www.animalplanet.com/monstersinsideus

Killing large brain parasites can cause the lymph nodes to swell, especially under the jaw, and sometimes encephalitis. So it is best to help this process in the patient by cleansing and exercise.

Fasciolopsis buski: This parasite lives where cancer is in the body, and alternative practitioners use the location of the parasite to determine where cancer is located. If we find it in the brain, we know the patient has brain cancer. No one with brain cancer has a functional brain because of the parasite, not because of the cancer.

Loa loa: This is a parasite that likes to reside in lymph nodes, optic nerve, skin, heart, and brain, and causes blindness, filiariasis, as well as massive skin problems.

Echinoporyphium recurvatum and echinostoma revolutum are parasites that attack the myelin sheath surrounding our nerve fiber, causing herpetic disease, Epstein Barr virus, sclerotic diseases amyotrophic lateral sclerosis, and multiple sclerosis. They are always in the brain, of course, as the brain is the switch board of our nervous system. The internet web sites list these as very rare parasites, and there is very little information available about them. They are listed by Clark as tropical parasites, but I have seen people in temperate climates with them. The worst case I have ever seen was in a woman in Los Angeles, California, who had such a tremendous amount of echinoporphyrium that she was collecting the parasites on cellophane tape as they emerged through the pores of her skin. When I applied frequency generation, the parasites began to emerge all over her forearms. She was literally crawling with parasites! Her brain was not working at all; she was totally dysfunctional and not able to work, drive, or do much of anything. This is the main cause of tremor. If people have these two parasites, coupled with the presence of shigella flexemi bacteria, they will shake uncontrollably. If an MD sees them they will probably be diagnosed with Parkinson's disease.

Cryptosporidium parasite can be anywhere in body, but usually prefers to live in men's prostate glands, which is the primary cause of prostatitis, and eventually prostate cancer. It also likes the bladder, and causes frequent urination and cancer of bladder, brain, etc.

Symptoms of Brain Parasitism

- Depression
- Dizziness when a person stands up.
- Headaches, extremely painful headaches
- Seizures
- Eye and vision problems
- Inability to focus the eyes
- Poor decision making
- Antisocial behavior

More research needs to be done. Zincrometer analysis is an essential skill for further research into the effects of parasites in the brain. It is not difficult to learn, but it requires years of practice to become proficient. I shared my knowledge with the world, as did Hulda Clark and many other brilliant health researchers. I taught zincrometer testing as well as practicing the technique. I tested saliva samples from all over the world; many of my patients I had never seen. They sent a sample; I tested it for hundreds of pathogens, wrote an email report of what they were positive for, and what disease they would have from the pathogens, and advised how to get rid of them and avoid them.

I tested and treated people wherever I went and found these pathogens common everywhere. I looked things up on the internet and frequently saw statements such as this: "This is a parasite which only exists in the tropics so little is known about it," as if to say no one should worry about this as it is NOT common. The world gets smaller every day, and people travel with their pathogens, spreading them around the world. I found "tropical" pathogens in all climates. I have not been to the South Pole, but I would expect to see the same things there that I see everywhere else.

Places to Look for Parasites

- Water: tap water, and still bodies of water.
- Rice from paddies where human feces are used to fertilize.
- Nuts should always be tested as the older they are the more likely to be contaminated.
- Bread (from the water used for baking).
- Ground, as in ascaris, which plagues gardeners since it can live dormant in soil for years.

- Tubers: potatoes, carrots (old carrots can carry all 6 of the main brain parasites), onions, beets, etc. are the source of Lyme disease, especially russet potatoes.
- Surfaces: bacteria live in clinics and hospitals that rely on antibiotics. I use colloidal silver water as a surface disinfectant to keep my clinic clean.
- People shaking hands, hugging, kissing
- Hand towels in bathrooms.
- Shared computer key boards, mice, etc.
- Bedding: many parasites come out of the body at night and lay eggs on the sheets.
- Clothing, especially what is worn to bed at night.
- Vegetables that are not prepared properly, such as cruciferous vegetables. Hydroponic vegetables will be positive for whatever the water used to grow them in is positive for.

Pets frequently carry many pathogens and should be wormed frequently, especially if they associate with other animals. Cats pass pathogens primarily through their feces. They defecate anywhere that they can find a little dirt to throw over their feces. People pick up these parasites and bacteria by handling or stepping in the cat feces. If cats are using a litter box, cleaning the box is a dangerous job that should be done very carefully. Rubber gloves and extreme hygiene are called for. Dogs pass pathogens mainly through their saliva, drooling, and licking their masters to show affection, passing pathogens to other mammals.

ARORANGI PRISON

As my knowledge increased with research and practice, I realized that mental disorders of all kinds were caused by parasites in the brain.

After I had proven these theories beyond any doubt, I had a conversation with the warden of our small island prison on Rarotonga. He felt most of the prisoners under his care seemed mentally handicapped. I offered to have a look at them, to Zincrometer diagnose and treat them at no charge. The warden accepted and I started volunteering at the prison one afternoon a week. They called me the "good Samaritan." My discoveries were exactly what I expected: every single prisoner I Zincrometer tested was positive for at least one brain parasite, and most had two or three parasites living in their brains.

The first inmate I tested had two brain parasites. When he was brought to me he could not focus his eyes; they were rolling around in his head. He was so withdrawn he did not know who he was, where he was, or who I was. Zincrometer test was positive for Toxoplasma gondii and Paragonimus westermani. I killed the parasites in his brain using varizapper frequency generator and the transformation was immediate; he looked at me with focused eyes, realized where he was and who he was, smiled at me, and thanked me profusely for helping him. Here was a young man who had a mental disorder from brain parasites and never should have been incarcerated; rather he should have had a medical evaluation before a hearing, pleading, or sentencing. The prison personnel watched this transformation and were amazed at the complete change in this young man's behavior. He had been in isolation because he had not communicated and they thought he might be violent; now he was smiling and talkative and not hearing voices in his head. The guard asked if he was OK to associate with other prisoners; I said now he was.

As I worked my way through the prison population, I saw the same pattern over and over again. If an MD or social worker or guard or anyone conversed with these inmates, they could tell that something was wrong with their mental processes. But their training would never help them diagnose the cause of the mental illness. A parasitologist, who could test, identify, and locate parasites, would be the only beneficial practitioner. This was knowledge that called for dissemination and was the catalyst for me to write a book. I had been speaking and lecturing at various venues on the island; and wherever I traveled, people were very responsive to my discoveries. They kept asking, "Why isn't something being done about the rehabilitation of these inmates?" Obviously if the inmates were returned to society without treating them for the cause of their incarceration, they would likely re-offend. This was a fatal flaw in the system. I have to assume that all prisons all over the world would be very similar. I continued this research.

Pure water to drink and food to eat at any prison must be available, or they will re-contaminate. Once a person has been infested with brain parasites, they have built a home in the brain. Care must be taken as any new parasite introduced can occupy the home and all symptoms return. Carrots that are not fresh are the main source of brain parasites and at Arorangi prison they were fed to the inmates!

TROPICAL DISEASES

Dengue is spreading all over the world, with numbers increasing steadily. It was named by the French when they attempted to build the Panama Canal. The English tried their hand at canal building next, and they lost many workers to the same malady, which they dubbed "break bone disease." The French and English suspected the disease was spread by mosquitoes. Americans were able to complete the Panama Canal by reducing mosquito numbers. Many assumptions have been made about this disease and most assumptions are wrong.

I had MDs tell me that there are four kinds of dengue and once people have had all four, they have permanent immunity from ever getting dengue again. I have tested positive for dengue dozens of times and expect to test positive many more times. Some say different types are more or less severe. In fact it is all the same; but if a person's defense systems are weak, the disease can be very severe. If health is good dengue symptoms are very mild. There is no immunity to dengue, malaria, Ross River virus, Barmah Forest fever, and many other tropical fever diseases. The mosquito bites you after it has bitten another with the disease, and you get the disease.

On a speaking tour in southern California in 2011, I was amazed that 10% of the people I tested on Zincrometer were positive for dengue. It was mid-winter there, and certainly not tropical, and I did not see a mosquito the entire time I was there. I assumed they had carried dengue for some time, or been infected by some other parasite and not the mosquito. Some would blame global warming for the spread of tropical diseases to temperate climates. I have come to the conclusion that travel is the culprit. I see epidemics spreading across areas one after another, as tourists bring diseases with them wherever they travel. If the tourists don't have it when they leave home, they stand a good chance of picking something up while sharing the same air as 300 people on an airplane.

Malaria, tuberculosis, and other fevers and respiratory diseases are spreading rapidly, as well. Doctors of internal medicine have no cure for any of these and no ability to deal with the overwhelming numbers of infected and sick. Zincrometer detection and frequency generation are the only hope at this time. It takes five minutes each to kill them with varizapper. If cytomegalovirus positive in the CNS it will hold the tropical diseases in the body; onco virus driver step 1 for the sv-40, then the frequencies for tropical positives and they will come out of CNS.

I remember in Viet Nam during the war, malaria tablets were being passed out every Monday morning, which caused unbelievable diarrhea by noon. Perhaps they thought they would flush us out? No one took the tablets more than once. I was positive for malaria a few years ago on a trip to a temperate climate and had not been visited by a mosquito. Probably ascaris carried malaria to me, as that was the only parasite I had in my body. It was an interesting experience because of the symptoms I developed; I zapped it out in five minutes. Alternative health care can cure these "tropical" diseases easily, but standard practice cannot. Malaria is endemic in tropical areas worldwide and will soon be endemic everywhere. See a naturopath if you get the symptoms.

WEIGHT LOSS

Weight problems can be discussed forever. Some people spend a great deal of their time worrying and talking about weight. The program below that I give to patients who want to lose weight works very well. But once a person stops eating processed foods, the weight comes off by itself. Unnatural fats from processed foods, especially polyunsaturated oils, are what have been causing people to put on weight all over the world. My waist size today is the same size it was when I stopped growing at about the age of 18. Between now and then, my waist slowly increased over the years, adding several inches until I changed my diet and lifestyle in my late 50s; from then on my waist diminished, until it was back to my teenage size, where it stays. One of the best habits I adopted was to ingest cinnamon every morning. I tried many ways to use cinnamon in baked goods, porridges, on bread, etc. I settled on beverage as the best delivery system. Cinnamon dissolves nicely in honey, so it is easy to add cinnamon to honey, and stir the honey into tea or other hot beverages. Just a pinch of cinnamon honey every morning curbs the appetite all day. I eat a small breakfast, no lunch, an early dinner, and a piece of fruit as a snack in the evening. I am never terribly hungry, my weight stays the same, and I store very little fat.

I worked with some very large people, 400 to 500 pounds; these people harbored the parasite echinococcosis (tape worm), which they got from eating watermelon, or from their overweight pets. This is a parasite which gathers fat and holds it, so these people cannot lose weight, no matter how hard they try; and even when they stop eating, they cannot lose. Once we detected and killed this parasite (and they wormed their pets that gave it to them), they lost weight rapidly. Overweight means faulty diet.

Farmed fish and aquaculture byproduct fluazinam create radiation buildup in the thyroid. The thyroid controls body mass, and if contaminated cause either hypo or hyper thyroidism. People either waste away or get huge. Asbestos accumulates in thyroid as well and it is very difficult to get rid of. This is the cause of chronic weight problems.

WEIGHT LOSS PROGRAM

1. Hoodia Gordonii or L-glutamine 2 capsules/day taken just before the 2 main meals each day.
2. Flax seed or coconut oil daily with either of the supplements for rapid weight loss.
3. Recommend liver cleanse to start.
4. Green tea stimulates fat burning.
5. Heat stimulates weight loss; eat chili, cayenne pepper, ginger, and turmeric.
6. Vinegar with meals helps burn fat; a tablespoon of wine vinegar or apple cider vinegar with each meal, as in olive oil and vinegar salad dressing.
7. Diet should consist of mainly raw foods. Eat as little cooked foods as possible. Butter and coconut oils are best; avoid all polyunsaturated oils and spreads like margarine and soy cooking oils.
8. Eat nothing from a can except sardines. No corned beef, salmon, or shrimp or prawns (farmed fish), ham or bacon. Avoid all fried chicken outlets.
9. Always eat breakfast. Never eat after 6 pm at night. Make mid-day meal the main meal of the day.

10. Fresh grapefruit or juice helps burn fat and protects against diabetes by lowering glucose and insulin levels.
11. Squeeze an ear lobe between thumb and finger for one minute just before eating. This acupressure technique curbs appetite.
12. Use no pots or pans with Teflon coating; Teflon sheds thallium and gold which make shins ache and causes obesity.
13. Cinnamon curbs appetite; ½ teaspoon mixed with 1 teaspoon of honey daily.
14. This program is designed to help you reach your ideal weight and also improve your health. Herbal supplements suppress appetite, increase metabolism, burn calories, and increase energy.
15. Check thyroid thoroughly and remove all pathogens from it as the thyroid gland controls body mass.
16. For those who wish to lose weight rapidly, daily exercise for 30 minutes and flax seed oil are highly recommended.

HEAVY METAL REMOVAL

No heavy metal should be anywhere in the human body. If we are over 50 years of age, we probably have, or have had, amalgam fillings in our teeth that contain mercury and nickel. I had 18 at one time and have had them all removed over the years. This is the main cause of mercury poisoning worldwide. The highly advertised study paid for by the American Dental Association, claiming that tuna fish were poisoning us with mercury, was very effective at casting the blame elsewhere, but the fact of the matter is that I have never tested tuna that was positive for mercury. One of the exercises we did for the Clark seminar in Australia in 2008 was to procure samples of fish from mongers around Sydney, Australia, and test them for pathogens. We found plenty of parasites but no heavy metals.

Mercury is a major factor in assault, spousal abuse, child abuse, etc., because it makes us tense, easy to anger, and strike out. Can't sleep at night or relax during the day? Suspect mercury poisoning. Nickel usually accompanies mercury and it is used to make things shiny, like stainless steel cutlery. If you place a stainless steel knife in a jar of mayonnaise for one minute, it will turn black as the acidic mayo is leeching the nickel out. Nickel destroys our kidneys. Mercury and nickel are frequently in tap water.

Worldwide, the most dangerous heavy metal that is spreading rapidly is thallium. One drop of thallium ingested will kill you in minutes. It is conductive and used in circuitry, so endangers technicians who come in contact with it repairing electronics; but the main source of contamination is from Teflon coated cookware. I tell all patients to throw away any Teflon coated pots, pans, baking dishes, etc. Many of the small islands are atolls with no ground water, so they catch water from the roofs of their houses. This works well where it rains most days, but if the roof is made of aluminium there is a problem. When salt sits on aluminium it draws the aluminium out in powder; oxidation. Then new rain washes the aluminium powder into the storage tank. It is okay to bath with it, but if we drink the water we get aluminium poisoning, which causes Alzheimer's disease and heart disease.

METAL REMOVAL RECIPE PROTOCOL

Best done after liver and kidney cleansing.

- Thioctic acid (250mg) 2 daily for 3 weeks
- MSM (650mg) 3 daily for 2 months...
- Glutathione (500mg) 3 daily for 3 weeks.
- Magnesium oxide (300mg) 1 evening for 3 weeks
- Thallium removal with L-glutamine; one tablet with each meal.

Seaweed or supplements made from it like chlorella and selenium; remove heavy metals.

NERVE DISEASES

Scientists and doctors love to name things. They are constantly coming up with more and more exotic diseases with odd names (the discoverer-describers get their name in there somehow). When it comes to nerve diseases, it gets ridiculous. Parkinson's, epilepsy, sclerosis, tremor, epilepsy, fibromyalgia. A new description comes out with a new name constantly, but they are all describing the same thing. Nerve disease is parasitic and sometimes exacerbated with bacteria or virus. Period. Echinostoma revolutum, echinoporphyrium recurvatum, and gastrothylax elongates are the parasites; and shigella flexemi is the odd bacteria. When I locate and eradicate these parasites and this bacterium, improvement is immediate. Ascaris, Naegleria fowleri, xylene, tuolene, and nocardia asteroids are triggers; and magnesium deficiency must be considered. Epstein Barr virus is carried by Echinoporphyrium and a cause of chronic fatigue syndrome, as well as all herpetic disease (herpes) which is very curable; but MDs say that there is NO cure for herpes. This very common parasite, echinoporphyrium recurvatum, is the main pathogen that lowers our immune system capability. If you look it up on the internet you will see statements like: "This is a rare parasite that not much is known about." You must look for something to find it and see how common it actually is. Most people with AIDS harbor this parasite. It welcomes all pathogens by lowering immunity in its host, especially STDs. It can reside anywhere as it lives on the myelin sheath which surrounds nerve fiber and follows nerves all over the body. If it is in the pancreas it causes symptoms that are mistaken for diabetes.

Asbestos located in the central nervous system? Tremor will always be there until all asbestos has been removed.

Nerve patients are the most difficult to treat of any patients because the treatments are electricity generation, which can cause them pain; and since they live with lots of pain all the time, they don't want anything that causes more pain. Plus they are confused, as the parasites are always in the brain. They require a great deal of counseling. Once the pain-bringing bacteria is gone, the causative parasites are killed, and toxins removed, they finally get their feet on the ground and start to make sense.

BETTER HEALTH RESEARCH CENTRE PROTOCOL FOR HERPETIC DISEASE AND NERVE PROBLEMS

1. Zincrometer test positive for echinoporphyrium recurvatum and or echinostoma revolutum.
2. Verizapper with ALS or MS driver, steps 10 and 11.
3. Recheck for parasites in muscle tissue, lungs, parotid and sublingual glands; still positive? Run steps again until negative.
4. Zincrometer test for Epstein Barr virus, herpes, and many STD's as they will be negative if you have killed the echinoporphyrium.
5. Zincrometer test for coxsackie brain viruses and papilloma warts virus as they are carried by the echinostoma; if not negative use common virus driver steps 8+10 to kill them.

All people that I have zincrometer tested positive for herpetic disease are also positive for echinoporphyrium and vice versa. This is a complete cure for herpetic disease.

All people that I have tested positive for echinostoma will also be positive for coxsackie and papilloma; this is a complete cure for the brain virus and venereal warts.

Identify source to not re-contaminate: Zincrometer test all tubers and fruits. These parasites are in the environment and food chain; oranges, mangos, cabbage, water, etc.

Asbestos must be considered; liver cleanse can flush it but may take several to get it out of the nervous system.

PARKINSON'S DISEASE, SCLEROSIS, FIBROMYALGIA, AND EPILEPSY PROTOCOL

1. Biowave generation with ALS, MS, Parkinson's or epilepsy driver daily for 2 weeks; then once or twice a week for maintenance.
2. Test for parasites in brain and nervous system, especially ascaris, echinostoma, echinoporphyrium, and Naegleria fowleri infestation in the brain, and Xylene, Tuolene, or PCP toxicity.
3. Hulda Clark states that Parkinson's is caused by staphylococcus infection. Nocardia bacteria usually introduced during dental work, particularly during wisdom tooth removal. Dental clean up indicated; no amalgam fillings. Hulda also stated that there is a connection between herpes virus and epilepsy. I found it! Echinoporphyrium recurvatum parasite carries Epstein Barr virus which is a herpetic virus. Once the echinoporphyrium is negative in the central nervous system, herpes, coxsackie, and EBV disappear from the body completely. CV steps 8+10

4. These diseases are usually accompanied by chronic constipation; cleanses are crucial, and good elimination is necessary (2 or 3 bowel movements/day). Magnesium levels in body must be raised; 300mg magnesium oxide, one in morning and one at night. Reduce dosage once bowels are regular (3 movements/day).
5. L-tryptophan; one capsule daily on empty stomach lessens shaking from Parkinson's.
6. Flax or coconut oil daily, 2 capsules or 2 tablespoons liquid. Eat lots of dark green leafy vegetables like turnip greens, spinach etc. Fresh, raw fruits, and vegetables daily. Cherries fresh or canned in their own juice
7. People who have seizures should never eat chicken or eggs or grapes or strawberries, as they contain malvin, which is a natural dye that can trigger seizures.
8. Boil all dairy products or zap with C. bacteria steps 5+8+9+10+11.
9. Niacin amide 500 mg 3 times daily to detoxify liver and do liver cleanse every 6 months; niacin amide counteracts ergot which is in some red wines and whole grains, which should be eliminated from diet; this will reduce seizure frequency.

10. Keep all pets outdoors and wash hands thoroughly with soap and disinfect if touching animals.
11. Toxin-free environment is crucial. Test coffee beans and all beans and nuts for mycotoxins, as they are frequently introduced in processing; or don't drink coffee or eat nuts or beans of any kind.
12. Listen to your body. It will tell you when you are about to have a seizure, so you can avoid having it. Common indicators are headache, nervousness, tingling or numbness, visual disturbances, twitching, flushing, metallic taste in the mouth. When symptoms are experienced, lie down in a darkened room, clear the mind and try to take a nap (relax), and use generator with epilepsy driver.
13. Clearing of ascaris and Naegleria fowleri and dyes from the brain always stops seizures; Homeographic remedies of malvin on page 376 of Hulda Clark's *Prevention of All Cancer* book. Or use cancer or common parasite driver to kill ascaris and take selenium to remove dyes from cranium.
14. Green tea, 2 to 4 cups daily, stops brain cell deterioration and causes regeneration of nerve tissue.

15. Check for MSG—a major factor in this disease, according to Mercola.
16. Shigella flexemi also causes tremors, and it is in most tomatoes and peppers, and all eggplant.
17. Chronic fatigue syndrome is very interesting. Hulda wrote that it was probably from tapeworm or ascaris; but I discovered that echinoporphyrium was the carrier of Epstein Barr virus, and the combination of virus and parasite was the real cause. When dealing with this syndrome you must look for echinoporphyrium in the central nervous system; place echino test vial on right plate of zincrometer and CNS vial on left side; if positive place EBV test vial on right plate and it too will be positive. Apply frequency 421 with ALS or MS driver. Retest for echino in CNS, parotid and sublingual glands, and muscle tissue; if negative, EBV will also be negative. This is herpes and mononucleosis as well as sclerosis and a factor in anemia. Vitamin D deficiency invites these maladies. All hepatitis is brought by parasites; see section on this.

LYME DISEASE?

Lyme disease is another name-in-lights scenario. The original research and naming was unbelievably flawed. Lyme decided that this was a disease common to the New England area of North America, which was acquired when a human being was bitten by a certain tick, which lived on the back of a certain type of deer. If this tick bit the deer, drawing blood, and then bit a human, the human would get the disease. After outbreaks in Europe, and all over the world where this deer and tick do not exist, most realized that something was wrong with this conclusion. There are still some people who believe the research, and a lot of other wrong info on the internet.

In dealing with an epidemic of Lyme in the Cook Islands, where we had no deer or ticks, I had to figure out what was really going on. After seeing a few dozen people with the symptoms, it was easy to see what was happening. All tested positive for ascaris parasite, and the bacteria and viruses present were carried by the ascaris. I proved this to myself, as I saw that the bacteria could not be killed unless the parasite was killed first. Once I was sure the parasites were all dead, I could easily kill the Bacteroides fragilis, borrelia borgdorferi, and coxsackie viruses. Occasionally the ascaris also carried Chlamydia, and it could not be eradicated without first killing the parasite carrier, either. Sometimes ascaris also brought streptococcus pneumonia, and it behaved in the same way. Once I knew what was actually happening I could cure Lyme completely in less than one hour. Varizapper with common parasite, bacteria, and virus drivers. Then I looked for the sources in my environment; tubers! Potatoes, onions, beets, carrots, etc. imported from New Zealand.

HEART DISEASE

ANGINA

Another set of lifestyle diseases is that dealing with our circulatory systems, our body's ability to circulate oxygenated blood to feed our cells. If respiration is good, our hearts are re-infused with newly oxygenated blood with each beat. Our kidneys regulate heart action, for example by regulating our blood pressure. Kidney health is very important to heart health, just as respiration is. If our kidneys are clogged with heavy metals, mold, and chemicals, or radiation, our heart health deteriorates. It is essential that all of our organs are working together, and not handicapped by pathogens, for overall good health. Cleansing our filters regularly is imperative to remove pathogen accumulation there. Liver cleanses, kidneys cleanses, water flushes, seaweed in all its forms, etc. But if we avoid foods containing pathogens, our filters are not burdened with too much to do in the first place.

No parasites in heart? Place muscle or heart slide on left side of zincrometer; nocardia asteroids and staphylococcus aureus on right side. If positive kill these bacteria that cause heart disease, edema, and congestion around heart and other organs. Where do we get these bacteria? They live at the dentist's and doctor's office. We get heart disease from office visits as this surface bacteria cannot be killed with antibiotics. Also in the food chain; peppers are a frequent carrier.

Angina is caused by zinc deficiency, so we must insure adequate supply of zinc in diet. Seeds and nuts eaten regularly will do it. If a person has angina, see below recipe:

ANGINA

The mineral zinc can cure angina quickly using Dr. David Williams' recipe below:

Body weight:

60 kg (or 132 pounds)	three 50 mg tablets/day
90 kg (or 198 pounds)	four 50 mg tablets/day
120 kg (or 264 pound)	five 50 mg tablets/day
150 kg (or 330 pounds)	six 50 mg tablets/day

These dosages should be lowered as soon as the angina pain disappears, usually within 7 days. Maximum period should be 14 days.

If individual is low in copper, take 4–6 mg of copper daily for 14 days prior to zinc program.

Eat seeds and nuts frequently as they contain zinc.

HIGH BLOOD PRESSURE

Blood pressure regulation is a huge business for big pharm, garnering billions of dollars in revenue yearly. If we kept our kidneys clean and functioning, we would not need all of this blood pressure medication. With haemopholis in our water supplies, it is difficult to avoid its accumulation in our kidneys and that raises our blood pressure. Removing haemopholis with frequency generation lowers blood pressure. It is in the water, so it gets into bread and whatever we cook in tap water. In other words, our environment must be free of these pathogens. They can all be killed with frequency generation, but better we fix them before we ingest them. If a person can Zincrometer test and find what pathogens are present, they can be killed before we drink, eat, cook with, bath in, etc. I test water, bread, vegetables, eggs, meats, fish, etc. Removal of pathogens means my family and I need very little treatment ourselves, because we have cleaned up the pathogens around us. Extreme hygiene? It is worth it.

Molds carry the mycotoxins that affect the kidneys. Most baked goods will test positive for several molds.

Zearalenone is the most difficult to kill and it is in bread, biscuits, cookies, beans, pasta, etc. Find it and kill it and kidneys will function better and blood pressure will become normal. The bags under eyes indicate sluggish kidneys; as we remove molds the eyes will look better, so we can watch this area of the body to see improvement. Common fungi driver in verizapper.

Ascaris is the parasite that can raise blood pressure, so we must always be diligent in its elimination. But any parasite in kidneys can elevate blood pressure; entamoeba which carries hepatitis E is another to look for. Herpetic disease raises blood pressure; killing echinostoma and echinoporphyrium drops the pressure. Paragonimus westermani parasite sometimes inhabits the pituitary gland and adrenal glands which control kidneys and cause high BP especially in mornings. Kidney zincrometer analysis will identify what is in kidneys, adrenals and pituitary; zapper will kill or neutralize the pathogen and the pressure will normalize.

Radiation should not accumulate in our bodies. If it tests positive in kidneys it must be removed to lower BP. Don't eat farmed fish; it is all radioactive: salmon, shrimp, krill, prawns, etc. Most canned fish is not edible. Fish oil is dangerous; never take it. Radioactive bromine from aquaculture causes thyroid, heart, kidney, etc. diseases. In 2012, a woman in her sixties ate an entire bag of frozen prawns. She almost died that night. Her blood pressure was over the moon, and she experienced multiple symptoms from her heart, kidneys, and thyroid. It took 6 months to leach the farmed fish toxins from her body.

Chemicals, herbicides, fungicides from agriculture come to us from eating foods that were sprayed with these chemicals. Eat organic but always test for these in body filters.

All blood pressure drugs have multiple side effects the worst of which is sterility. Most BP lowering meds that are generic; they are made with bromine, which is radioactive and will actually raise BP instead of lowering it. When we clean up our kidneys sexual function returns.

Benzene in kidneys is another pathogen that raises blood pressure. Hulda stated that benzoic acid preservative is the problem here. Citric acid is a better preserver in soft drinks. Some manufacturers use both; and when citric and benzoic meet, they produce benzene. It must be removed to get kidneys functioning and BP lowered. Zappication will help but liver cleansing as soon as detected is best.

HIGH BLOOD PRESSURE – HYPERTENSION PROTOCOL

1. Biowave generation daily for 2 weeks using kidney, high blood pressure, common fungi, or allergy drivers. Then twice a week for maintenance.
2. Liver cleanse every 6 months.
3. Avoid refined salt, moldy coffee, black tea, alcohol, and high fructose corn syrup (the sweetener in most soft drinks). Eat or drink nothing that has been microwaved.
4. Increase consumption of vegetables and fruit; 4 celery stalks/day will lower blood pressure 13%. Turnips are the best vegetables to eat to lower blood pressure. Graviola (kataraapa, soursop, and custard apple) seeds crushed kill parasites; juice, fruit, and tea from leaves all lower blood pressure. Place 7 leaves between your pillow and the case to aid sleep, relaxation, lower stress, etc.
5. Dark chocolate: 10 small squares a day can lower blood pressure 15 to 20 points.
6. Reduce consumption of red meats.
7. Drink lots of purified or rain water and hibiscus flower tea or juice.

8. Prescribe flax seed oil, calcium, and magnesium. One capsule of tryptophan with a small glass of milk reduces blood pressure.
9. Practice relaxation: yoga, exercise, meditation, etc.
10. Enzyme CoQ10 daily
11. Bromelain cleans veins and arteries of plaque for better circulation; 2 tablets on an empty stomach in the am, mid-day, and the pm = 6 a day. Pycnogenol also helps circulation.
12. Exercise daily 30 minutes.
13. Use turmeric and cayenne pepper seasoning.
14. Diuretics cause diabetes; and if a patient already has diabetes, discontinue use. If edema (water retention) is a problem, the best natural diuretic is coconut milk, one glass a day.
15. Passion fruit or its juice lowers blood pressure.
16. Cinnamon removes LDL cholesterol; ½ teaspoons every morning in 1 teaspoon of honey. Nice with graviola leaf tea.
17. Avoid drinking tap water, eating bread made with tap water, cucumbers, etc. grown in tap water. Tap water frequently has bacteria that raises blood pressure.

Campylobacter, helicobacter, staph aureus, nocardia asteroides, and haemopholis invade kidneys, raising blood pressure.

18. Bromelain is an enzyme from the core of the pineapple. The Dole pineapple company noticed that none of their employees had atherosclerosis; but the incidence in the Hawaiian people was very high. They hired scientists to find out why this was the case. The researchers found that the Hawaiians working in the fields for Dole were consuming pineapple as they worked. Now we can get the enzyme in tablet form: bromelain. This particular enzyme when taken on an empty stomach digests fibrin. Fibrin is the glue that holds plaque in place in the arteries and veins. When bromelain dissolves the fibrin, the LDL cholesterol and triglycerides pass out of the blood stream. No more plaque builds up. Works hundreds of times better than statins, with no deleterious side effects. Bromelain is a natural enzyme occurring in fruit, so it cannot be patented; there is no profit for big pharm.
19. For prevention, test for and kill all molds in your water and food.

20. Make sure there are no parasites, bacteria, or toxins in the kidneys, adrenals or pituitary.
21. Test for radiation in kidneys; Zappication to neutralize, chlorella (seaweed), vitamin D from sun daily, and cleanses to remove.

STROKE

A stroke is a warning from our body, telling us that we have mold in our blood. Sorghum mold is the cause of stroke. Obviously the mold must be killed and quickly, or the body will talk to us again with another stroke, and it is usually the second or third stroke that causes death. Stroke is easily prevented by insuring that we ingest no moldy sugar. White sugar, brown sugar, honey, etc. All sweeteners will go moldy. Vitamin C kills mold. When I buy a packet of sugar or any sweetener I add a level teaspoon of vitamin C powder to it and shake it up and keep in the refrigerator. If we zap sweeteners with common fungi driver step 7 we can kill sorghum mold in 5 minutes. My family and I never test positive for sorghum mold. My father and grandfather died of stroke; I do not intend to.

One day at the clinic I was seeing two patients when the phone rang. I answered and heard slurred speech, but I recognized the voice and said his name. I heard grunted agreement. I hung up, told my patients I had an emergency and would return shortly. I ran to my vehicle and raced to his house nearby. He was sitting in the kitchen with half of his body paralyzed. He was trying to talk but gibberish was coming out. Zincrometer test for mold was positive; I used the generator to kill the mold. I saw a papaya on the kitchen counter by the blender. I peeled the green parts off the papaya and discarded them and put rest of papaya and one peeled banana into the blender. After it was processed, I gave a large glass of the mixture to the patient. Minutes later as the generator finished killing the mold in his body, and vitamin C and Papain were working, he recovered completely in minutes and said clearly, "I feel great; I had better get to work." If everyone followed this procedure, we would have no more death or paralysis from stroke. Unfortunately, most people would call an ambulance.

STROKE OR HEART ATTACK PROTOCOL

1. Test for sorghum mold most likely in the brain; use common fungi driver step 7 to kill it.
2. Test for heartworm (dirofilaria immitis) and loa loa; use heart driver step 1+2 to kill them.
3. Discover how the sorghum mold is introduced to body; usually it is through a sweetener, especially brown sugar. Remove from diet. A teaspoon of vitamin C powder added to a packet of sugar, mixed well to kill the mold.
4. Check pets for heartworm; worm pets.
5. Give niacin immediately after stroke, followed by bromelain.
6. During recovery use allergy driver to rebuild immune system.
7. Eat lots of fresh fruit for vitamin C. Passion fruit is highest in vitamin C.
8. Dramatically reduce consumption of red meats, as amino acid homocysteine will build up in body causing heart disease of many types. B vitamins reduce homocysteine levels.
9. Test for and kill all molds using common fungi driver.

DIGESTION PROBLEMS

Digestion is an enormous problem for many people, and it is increasing as we eat more and more processed foods full of chemicals. Pernicious anemia is a major factor, for which there is a hereditary predisposition in some cases. But basically, bad habits and exposure to pathogens are the main causes. Anemia leads to IBS/Crohns, and that leads to arrhythmia, which leads to heart failure: Death. Simple ingestion of the chemical MSG can and does kill these people. Why do some countries still allow MSG in food? Unbelievable but true. Most developed countries simply regulate MSG and require manufacturers to warn of its presence on the labeling. It should be completely illegal everywhere. The facts are well known, but action is limited because it helps vendors sell "tenderized" products, and of course MSG increases appetite, so the customer will purchase more food. It is great for the vendor but life threatening for the consumer.

The shigella bacteria's are frequently in dairy products. Shigella sonei is the main cause of stomach pain.

Shigella dysenteriae is the main cause of bowel problems.

Shigella flexemi is the cause of tremor. The cow's tail getting into the milk? Dairy products frequently test positive for shigellas. Especially block cheeses. If I purchase butter, cheese, or any cow's milk dairy, I apply the frequencies to kill shigella before consumption. Goat's milk is the best way to take dairy. I love feta cheese from goats, and it is conducive to longevity.

Carbohydrate digestion takes place primarily in the mouth. Our saliva transforms the starch into sugar. But if we wash the carb down with liquid prior to transformation; the starch gets to the liver bile at the bottom of the stomach, and this impedes digestion and elimination. Never put liquid on the table when your family eats. Drink liquids after eating—never with food. Wine is an exception as most people sip wine and don't gulp it down with food. Wine improves the taste of many foods.

Fish poisoning is nothing new. It has been around since man has been eating the fish. Fish have their own pathogens, just like mammals do. All primitive societies developed methods to deal with fish parasites. Europeans usually just use heat, cooking the fish to kill its pathogens, which is not very effective, and of course overcooked protein is not as tasty. Polynesian people use lemon or lime to kill parasites in fish. Japanese use wasabi and ginger. These days many cooks have decided that fish should be seared on the outside of the fillet, and left raw on the inside; perhaps this improves taste to someone? It is a very dangerous way of preparing fish as the parasites are left alive and ready to proliferate in the consumer. Fish is a very good source of protein, but we should treat it, or cook it properly, so that it doesn't give us pathogens. Fish parasites are dangerous over time, but fish toxin ciguatera effects are instant. Ciguatera is poison and it is cumulative; the more you ingest the sicker you become. Parasites can be zapped and killed quickly, but ciguatera must be leeched out of the body and organs that it has poisoned. A bad case of fish poisoning can take the body years to recuperate from.

DIGESTIVE PROBLEMS PROTOCOL

As in fish poisoning or other toxic overload:

1. Biowave generation with colitis/ibs driver until relieved.
2. Avoid all onion and garlic, Lilly family foods; especially raw.
3. Eat fruit and vegetables; yogurt, prunes, papaya are best.
4. Prescribe digestive enzymes, one with each meal.
5. Green tea as needed to sooth stomach.
6. Avoid coffee, black tea, alcohol, caffeinated beverages.
7. Cruciferous vegetables (cabbage family) must be thoroughly cooked to be digested. Cabbage, broccoli, cauliflower, kohlrabi, Brussels sprouts. Never eat these raw, as they contain cyanide and fungi.
8. Eat nothing from a lagoon.
9. Selenium; 4 tablets am, and 4 tablets pm, for a few days; then gradually reduce to 1 tablet am and 1 tablet pm until jar is emptied.
10. Vitamin B-6 same as selenium.
11. For itching skin, soak in a tide pool in reef at low tide, or ½ cup of Epsom salts in a basin applied liberally over skin

and air dry. G-5 liquid sprayed on skin relieves itching in minutes.

12. If positive for metagonimus yokogawa or clonorchis sinensis parasites, use common parasite driver or colitis driver.
13. Coconuts are a natural source of selenium and germanium; eat fresh coconut or coconut cream. Any seeds and nuts supply these natural helpers.
14. Check for mycotoxins; if coffee drinker, look for mold in coffee. Best for people with digestive problems to avoid coffee and black tea, beans, onions, bread, and pasta or zap them with fungi frequencies.
15. Echinoporyphium and echinostoma must be eliminated if positive on zincrometer; they cause spastic colon and I suspect anemia as well. More research needs to be done on these parasites.

CHRONIC FATIGUE, LIVER DISEASE, HEPATITIS

World Health Organization: WHO is concerned as hepatitis is on the rise worldwide, western medicine cannot cure hepatitis, and their scientists don't know what causes it or where it comes from. I test for hepatitis A, B, C, D, E, F, and G, and look for the carriers of these types of hepatitis.

- Hepatitis A is carried by heartworm (dirofillaria immitis).
- Hepatitis A and G are carried by loa loa parasites.
- Hepatitis B+C are carried by ascaris parasite.
- Hepatitis E+D are carried by Entamoeba coli.
- I have never tested anyone positive for hepatitis F so far.

Hepatitis is the main cause of liver disease and chronic fatigue. The carrying parasites must be killed to cure the hepatitis. Once the parasite has been killed application of hepatitis antigen frequency with CV step 12 or Tropical step 10 frequency 418 completely cures hepatitis and chronic fatigue. Since the carrying parasites are in our environment, they must be found and eliminated or reinfection will occur.

Loa loa and heartworm are usually spread by an insect bite from a mosquito so they must be killed. Ascaris usually from potato or other tubers. Entamoeba coli is in many vegetables. Zincrometer location and removal.

Another cause of chronic fatigue is heart congestion from nocardia asteroides, and staphylococcus aureus bacteria and other MRSA bacteria's.

PERNICIOUS ANEMIA PROTOCOL

Symptoms: Low blood pressure, light headedness, pale skin, tongue soreness around the edges, yellow eye whites, weakness and fatigue, difficulty breathing. The cause of anemia is pathogens in kidneys; usually ascaris parasites, fungi, mold, and the tropical parasites echinostoma and echinoporphyrium, campylobacter, and helicobacter pylori.

1. Biowave generation daily using liver driver followed by no driver for reinforcement for 2 weeks. Then twice weekly for maintenance.
2. Eat liver at least twice per week (pâté if you can't get fresh), and dark green leafy vegetables and fresh fruit.
3. Take vitamin B-12 and C and folic acid daily and iron, copper, and cobalt supplements.
4. Anemics should not eat honey or any high fructose corn syrup sweetener.
5. Anemia leads to IBS/Crohns disease (thinning of stomach lining), which leads to arrhythmia which can stop the heart from beating.

6. Must avoid MSG and other chemicals in food; best to eat at home and not eat out. Fresh vegetables, fresh fruit, fresh fish.
7. Eat lots of oily fish; mackerel, wild caught salmon, sardines. NO farmed fish.
8. Cinnamon is a good source of iron; ½ teaspoon every morning.

SKIN

Our skin is our largest and most abused organ. If we are healthy our skin is healthy. Feel good, look good. We spend a great deal of money and time trying to look our best. So we try all sorts of lotions, salves, and sun blocks, etc. Which mostly contain carcinogenic chemicals, which destroy our skin and give us skin cancer instead. If our diet is high in B vitamins, and we put nothing on it, we have beautiful skin. Not everyone likes to eat liver once a week, or consume bushels of dark green leafy vegetables. Fortunately the supplement niacin amide supplies all the vitamin B-3 that we need. I take 1000 mg of niacin amide every morning; and if I am out in the garden for many hours, I take another 500 mg tablet so that my skin will not burn. I have not had "sunburn" in many years because I have been taking niacin amide for many years. I used it to cure my rheumatoid arthritis, dissolve calcium deposits on my knuckles, and straighten my crippled fingers, and then realized that my skin had improved along with the arthritis. I love the stuff.

Most of the sun blocks, lotions, cosmetics, and salves on the market are very dangerous things to put on your skin.

Do the research with zincrometer, or buy Sanctum products from www.drclark.com.

Tomato, peppers, and eggplant (night-shade family) carry shigella flexemi, which cause itching and feeling as if something is crawling on your skin. Zap these vegetables with common bacteria step 9 before eating.

EDEMA (WATER RETENTION) PROTOCOL

Poor circulation is usually the cause. For better circulation (more oxygen delivered to extremities):

1. Bromelain; 6 tablets per day, 2 in morning, 2 mid-day and 2 evening between meals, on an empty stomach; eliminates swelling and reduces pain, removes plaque.
2. Biowave frequency generation using heart driver every other day.
3. Reflexology; massage left foot from under big toe to middle of foot. For fluid in lungs, massage top of foot between toes.
4. Low salt diet.
5. Elevate swollen limb.
6. Daily exercise, especially walking.
7. Liver and kidney cleanse or ginger, uva ursi, magnesium, and B-6 tablets daily.
8. If a person has cancer, test for malonic acid and azo dyes; Zappication to remove, but counsel as to what they are coming into the body from. Parsley tea can help, and lots of vitamin C.
9. Test for too much iron in blood: causes water retention.

10. Check for leprosy and TB.
11. Test for MRSA staphylococcus aureus and nocardia asteroids in muscle tissue.
12. Check for parasites, fungus, molds, and mycotoxins.
13. Detox foot patch overnight reduces edema very quickly. Or run c. fungi driver with gel pads affixed to feet

FERTILTY, LIBIDO, AND SEXUALLY TRANSMITTED DISEASES

Fertility and infertility are issues we must look at in different ways throughout our lives. A time for every purpose. Sometimes in our lives, the last thing we need is a child. At other times, a child can be the most desirable thing we could imagine. The main cause of infertility is sexually transmitted diseases, as they make the body unfit for child bearing, causing women to miscarry.

LIBIDO (SEXUAL FUNCTION) PROTOCOL

1. Healthy relationships are paramount! Affection, understanding, supportive, long-term loving relationships are the most important element of fulfilling sex.
2. Mental awareness: Talk to each other, spend time together, focus on the moment, and forget worries and business.
3. Sexy foods: Onions increase stamina and sexual vigor. Eggplant is very good for women. Figs, dates, cayenne pepper, parsley, ginger, and honey all help raise libido.
4. Herbs: ginseng, gingko, maca powder 1000 mg a day, tongkat Ali 100 mg each morning. We have found that Maca works best and it is affordable.
5. Improve circulation: bromelain, pycnogenol.
6. Longevity: Having sexual union 3 times per week promotes a long life. All people who live to more than 100 years have active sex lives.
7. Avoid antibiotics as they encourage STD activation, especially yeast, molds, and fungi.
8. Any parasites detected in men's prostate glands must be removed. The most common cause of prostatitis is

cryptosporidium, and it is present in all cases of prostate cancer that I have tested. Use common parasite driver step 6 with electrodes placed on either side of lower abdomen.

9. Echinostoma and echinoporphyrium tropical parasites invite STD's into the body. If detected early and killed, the STDs they carry with them will disappear without treatment. If they are in the body for any length of time, the pathogens carried by the parasites will become active and need treatment to get rid of them.
10. African chagas disease, brucellosis, is spreading worldwide. Brucella abortus bang should be tested for and killed or conception will be aborted.

SEXUALLY TRANSMITTED DISEASES

STDs should be better understood; there is an incredible amount of disinformation attached to them. "Sexually transmitted" is wrong, of course. STDs are all over in the environment, and intercourse is not the only way they are acquired. In fact, my experience is that they usually are NOT from intercourse. I have detected them in people who maintain that they are virgins. Small children who are definitely not sexually active frequently test positive for STDs. On the island of Rarotonga I tested the tap water every month. The pathogens changed from month to month; parasites, bacteria, etc. But always at least one STD and frequently many were present in the tap water. When I knew what is in the water, I knew what to expect my patients would test positive for.

Chlamydia was the most common disease in the Cook Islands and always positive in tap water. Back in the 1950s before the Cook Islands was an independent country, they were attached to New Zealand as a protector by England. New Zealand sent a team of "health care professionals" to the Cook Islands to determine why there was such a high incidence of chlamydia in these islands. The conclusion that the team came up with was that the people were extremely promiscuous. Over the next 60 years they would look at the issue over and over, and always come to the same wrong conclusion. They never bothered to look at the environment because chlamydia was an STD. If they had done any research they could have easily identified the source: water. Chlamydia is always in the tap water all year long, so of course at any given time, more than half of the population would test positive for the chlamydia.

Gardnerella vaginalis is another heat-resistant bacterium that is in tap water most of the time and most women there will test positive for it, as it can be acquired from bathing in the infected water. Boiling the water will not kill these heat-resistant bacteria. Trepanema pallidum is in the water about half of the time, so it is not as frequently seen in people, but since this is syphilis and capable of causing blindness and many other serious problems, it is not acceptable in tap water. The worst STD so far in the water is cytomegalovirus or SV-40. Simian virus-40 is one of the components for AIDS, which is why the incidence of AIDS was very high there. Benzene, which is another component of AIDS, is also sometimes in the tap water. Another is Paragonimus westermani which produces benzene.

Echinoporyphium parasite must be killed if positive as it carries STDs with it, along with Epstein Barr Virus and herpes. Once a person is negative for echino, many of the STDs will disappear without treatment.

I don't believe much of anything that MDs theorize about HIV and AIDS, as they have been completely wrong on all counts so far. The terms STDs, and the New Zealand nomenclature STIs, should be struck from the books. I don't know of any of these so-called sexually transmitted diseases that are only sexually transmitted. They are all on the rise, all over the world, because they are in our environment all over the world. These health-care workers with their bogus certifications and expert status need to go back to school, be re-educated, and taught to research, instead of blindly following the accepted position, which is so obviously erroneous. Since STDs lower immune system strength, they can open our bodies to all sorts of other pathogen acquisition. In countries that use bleach to purify water, I didn't find STDs in the water, but of course chlorine is a proven carcinogenic substance, so are we trading STD for cancer? Hulda Clark wrote about many of these issues and closed with the codicil "more research needs to be done" on these issues. I agree whole heartedly. My research in this area is very interesting, but I feel I have only scratched the surface.

CHILDRENS' DISEASES

I did a lot of work with children—newborn through puberty—and I saw the same pattern in all ages including adults. Tuberculosis of any kind opens the body to childhood diseases. A child or adult will also test positive for TB (it is the carrier) if he or she tests positive for any of the following:

- Chicken pox
- Measles
- Mumps
- Diphtheria
- Polio
- Rheumatic heart; strep veridans.

First identify what kind of TB; kill it, and the children's diseases that came with it can be easily conquered. Children's disease driver in varizapper; step 9 for the TB, followed by the frequency for the specific disease, or just run the entire driver. When adults get TB and children's diseases, the diseases can be far more serious. Mumps, for example, in men can cause infertility. I developed this theory many years ago, and have proven it many times over the years. This is completely at odds with accepted western medicine theory. It will be hard for many to accept. Try it, and see that it does work.

VACINATION

A vaccine is a weakened pathogen that is introduced to the human body with the idea that it will cause the body to build up a defense against the pathogen that will result in the body not acquiring the disease from the pathogen when next encountered. This is a theory that has been around for almost 100 years. It has been tried millions of times over the last 70 years. So far, no one has ever proven that any vaccination of any kind was ever of any benefit to anyone. Big pharm likes to mention polio in its defense, but this is a disease that ran its course and was in complete decline when the Salk vaccine was introduced to the world. The only thing that the Salk vaccine accomplished was to make sure that the disease continued to exist; it didn't cure anything but gave us AIDS from the vaccine. So why does big pharm continue to push this theory? Profit. They make millions every year with their bogus vaccine campaigns, and try to make the experiment mandatory for all.

There is no proof whatsoever of efficacy in vaccines, but there is a tremendous body of evidence that vaccines cause harm and do no good. Time to stop the profitable madness? Most scientists agree that this failed experiment has been very costly and should be stopped.

I received 9 mandatory shots in the US army in 1966 before I was sent to Viet Nam; I have not been able to sleep at night without help since that day. I have applied for military compensation but never received any to date.

I have a brother who has been dyslexic since the day he was vaccinated at age 6.

I have a son who has also been dyslexic since the day he was shot with Britain's BCG experiment on the colonies' children. He almost died from the shot and will never be 100% for the rest of his life.

Many patients I have seen have the same problem. Why? To profit big pharm, of course, and the governments that help pharm push the drugs benefit in taxes collected, so the madness continues.

Flu shots statistically increase the likelihood of contracting the flu dramatically, yet there are MDs out there that still recommend patients get a flu shot.

All vaccines carry many pathogens; mercury for example, is used because it helps the serum flow; mercury is deadly to the human body and it accumulates in organs and is hard to get out. Mercury poisoning is the main cause of spousal and child abuse. There are many more deadly ingredients in every shot. Vaccines are all bad; no good. No one in my family has had an injection of any kind since 1996, but we have had to fight school systems and governments to achieve this.

LONGEVITY

Bernard Jensen, the father of naturopathy, studied longevity extensively. He traveled around the world to every country that advertised people more than 100 years of age living there. He verified the records to insure they were actually more than 100. He asked them a series of questions, and then he compared the data. There were many things that they all had in common, to which Jensen attributed long life:

- Red grapes and or red wine; flavonoids in red grapes have often been identified as life extenders.
- Sardines; probably the fact that sardines are usually prepared with skin and oil in place; omegas in balance.
- Dairy as clabbered milk, cottage cheese from cows, or feta cheese from goats, and yogurt.
- Good air to breath; mountain valley away from cities, 2000 to 6000 feet above sea level.
- Active life; never retired, exercise from work.
- Alkaline; eat lots of fresh fruit and vegetables grown nearby.

- Baked goods made with pure water.
- Lots of water, as fresh from the sky as possible, with no chemicals in it.
- Olives; eaten and olive oil used in cooking.
- No one lives to these ages without a partner. Single people die young. Regular intercourse is the best exercise the human body can have.
- I would add the use of bromelain as plaque reduction is imperative to oxygen delivery to cells.

My father made it to 87; and when people asked him how he stayed so healthy he would say, "Just keep moving. If you stop moving you are dead." He walked two miles every morning and every afternoon. He also attributed his longevity to moderation, doing nothing in excess. His favorite saying was, "Each day I grow better and better," which was his father's mantra as well, since Grandpa learned it from the teachings of John Dewey during the great depression.

My mother died at 96, and I never saw her do any exercise, so I attribute her longevity to stubbornness (attitude).

Bernard Jensen died in his 90s. Many of my friends and acquaintances are studying longevity, and I think that in spite of the increasing pollution, and spread of pathogens, we will be able to beat the death march if we can locate and remove the problems. If we continue to wear blinders and accept wrong opinions, we will die young.

LONGEVITY PROTOCOL

"Life is an integration of enzyme reactions. Life ends when the worn out metabolic enzyme activity of the body drops to such a low point that it is unable to carry on vital enzyme reactions. Old age and debilitated metabolic enzyme activity are synonymous. If we postpone the debilitation of metabolic enzyme activity, what we now call old age could become the glorious prime of life!"

~ Dr. Edward Howell, *Enzyme Nutrition*.

1. Eat real sardines frequently.
2. Take dairy as clabbered milk (yogurt or cottage cheese).
3. Live in a mountain valley between 2000 and 6000 feet above sea level.
4. Regular sex at least twice a week.
5. Stay active, never retire, and exercise daily.
6. Stay alkaline; eat lots of fresh fruit and vegetables grown nearby.
7. Drink lots of water that is as fresh from the sky as possible with no chemicals in it.
8. Eat olives and use olive oil for cooking.

9. Eat red grapes and or drink red wine frequently.
10. Use bromelain enzymes for clearing arteries and veins of plaque.

CONCLUSION

"Don't go near the water!" That's what the Beach Boys sang back in the 1960s. All the talk and energy that has gone into saving the planet for the last 50 years has only scratched the surface, and the surface is the only illusion most people want to see. Beneath the surface we are in big trouble. The sky may look cleaner, and the water may look clearer. When we test the air and water we realize how bad it is, and getting worse, not better. Tropical diseases are spreading to temperate climates, and temperate diseases are spreading to tropical environments. Fifty year ago we assumed the problem was toxicity. Now we know that viruses, bacteria, parasites, mold, and fungi are winning the battles and we are losing. Not only do we need to take responsibility for our own bodies and health, we also must expand our context to include the planet we dwell on. We must all take responsibility for EARTH. Look around and see what you can do in your own environment.

Big business saturates the media with misinformation and outright lies. Consumer protection agencies must be insulated from the influence of big business, and big money, and encouraged to actually protect consumers. Drug companies need to be scrutinized and all drugs need to be tested on zincrometer before taking them; as faulty manufacturing practices mean many drugs are dangerous (look for radiation in many medications, as well as bromine which is the cause of thyroid problems). None of this will do anything if we don't also fix our judicial system. Legislation must be for the people, not for business interests.

We must stop putting our youth in prison and instead restore their health, so that they are good citizens of the world.

Regulation of insurance companies might work but I doubt it. Health care cannot be entrusted to insurance companies with their profit motives. I don't like the idea of socialized medicine because I grew up with brainwashing to adore capitalism, but government-run health care may be the only thing that works. What we have now is not working, so we must try other methods.

Politicians love to talk about the necessity for growth. Sustainability is a catch phrase that they all spew, as well. The thinking is that if we have growth we can continue to spend more and more money on nothing. Growth is not necessary! It has nothing to do with happiness. What the world's leaders should be focusing on is the environment. Environmental degradation will thwart any growth from being beneficial. If we improve the world environment real growth will occur by and of itself, because we will all be healthier and our brains will all work better, so that we can be more productive, and live longer in good health to be productive longer.

Wherever I travel, I test the tap water, bottled water, and food. My expectations were that I would find different pathogens in different environments. Patterns emerged which were surprising. For example, in California on a speaking tour, I tested water north of Los Angeles, south of Los Angeles, and in the center of the city. Results were about the same all over the area. Chlorine dioxin, of course, but haemopholis and meningococcus bacteria were there, along with poly chloral by phenols, fungi, and mold. All city water seemed to test this way in every city that I looked at. No wonder so many people suffer from arthritic symptoms. PCBs and chlorine are carcinogens so cancer of course starts there. In water that is not chlorinated the most unexpected pathogens I find are listed as sexually transmitted diseases. Gardnerella vaginalis, chlamydia, Trepanema pallidum (syphilis), and sometime cytomegalovirus (SV-40 a component of AIDS).

Bottled water was sometimes very pure and pathogen free, but some bottled water tested worse than tap water. Obviously not enough attention is given to quality of tap or bottled water. Is anyone testing bottled water anywhere in the world? Bottled water from developing country New Zealand contained asbestos and heavy metals mercury, chromium, and nickel. Water from Fiji contained these same pathogens and also aluminum. I tested the tap water monthly on my island, and the pathogens differed from month to month. I sent reports to government and worked with them to improve our water. Bottled water sold and produced in the Cook Islands was hit and miss; some was just tap water in a bottle, which is not potable, and even the one company that ozonated and was very careful did not always get it right. I told my patients to collect rain water for drinking, which is water from God's lips to yours. Hulda Clark recommended the same as she suspected all city water was not fit to bathe in much less drink. Take Gardnerella vaginalis for example; if a woman washes her private parts with water that has this bacterium in it, she is likely to introduce this bacterium, which causes the vagina to smell like rotten fish. Urinary dysfunction is something that most women in this country can expect as they age, since giardia lamblia and cryptosporidium parasites are in the water and easily infect the bladder, reducing volume capability and causing frequent urination. Fortunately, I can Zincrometer test and identify what is in the water and fix it with frequency generation. I can kill the parasites, bacteria, and neutralize some toxins, but heavy metals must be removed in other ways.

Tourism is the most likely cause of the spread of disease. In the Cook Islands, we had one epidemic after another, all year long, as tourists brought their sickness with them and spread it wherever they traveled. Airplanes are by far the most dangerous means of travel, when you consider that about 300 people are sharing the same air. In 2011, the flooding in Australia's Queensland caused mosquito populations to sore, and the odd Australian diseases, Ross River virus, Barmah Forest fever, Q-fever , burgeoned, then spread to New Zealand, then to the Cook Islands with tourists. A new epidemic started before its predecessor had finished. These many diseases not being indigenous to the area are a huge problem, since they were not suspected, and could go unrecognized until someone realized what they were and identified them.

What can we do? If we can afford an investment of a few hundred dollars in equipment, and take the time to learn how to use it, we can clean up our immediate environment to help our families. Then look around in your environment and find something you personally can do for others. I did house calls to the elderly and gave free diagnoses. I volunteered at the local prison. I did a great deal of work for no pay. As public service makes for a better community for all, we should all do it.

If we are serious about good health and longevity, we must start with ourselves, of course, and then constantly expand our context, to include more and more responsibility for more and more people, places, etc. From me to my family, to my tribe, to my town, country, continent, planet, solar system, universe!

FOOD AND WATER PURIFICATION

Purification of our environment should start with what we put inside of ourselves; breathing the best air that we can. Then liquid quality – water and any other beverage we consume. Food is the most difficult unless we have learned to Zincrometer test. Knowledge of what might be where gives us a head start as we learn Zincrometer. When you know what is in the water in your tap or bottle, you can zap the water with the frequencies to kill the pathogens you have discovered. Bread can carry parasites, bacteria, and mold if baked with water that had the pathogens. If we look at root crops like potatoes, carrots, onions, etc., we are likely to be dealing with molds; use common fungi driver to purify. Dairy is frequently contaminated with common bacterium shigella. Beans and pasta may contain mold, and coffee beans need to be tested for mold, too, and all grains. Rice is frequently contaminated with human parasites if human feces are used to fertilize.

Sept 19, 2011 my family was sickly after eating a dinner of fish and rice with coconut cream. The leftovers I tested were positive for clostridium botulinum, clostridium tetani, E, coli, all mycotoxins and their carrier aspergillus, staph aureus, and one parasite; enterobius vermicularis (pin worm). I zapped myself and the uncooked rice left in the bag. None of the pathogens would come out until I killed the pin worm; then the pathogens were killed, so I knew it was the parasite that was carrying the pathogens.

At home I place gel pads on dairy, produce, water, bread etc. Then I use common bacteria driver to kill bacteria I have identified with Zincrometer in dairy. In water and bread, mold and fungi are the carriers that bring parasites, bacteria, and viruses with them; common fungi driver step 1 and 2 kill the mold and the other pathogens will no longer test positive on zincrometer.

The better people are at Zincrometer identification, the better they will be at purifying their intake. The sick and dying especially must look at prevention as their immune systems are too weak to protect them. AIDS patients, for example, have to be very careful to avoid the mold zearalenone as it affects Paragonimus westermani parasite's ability to produce benzene, which activates the AIDS. Zearalenone is frequently in root crops, beans, pasta, and junk food.

WHAT I USE AT BETTER HEALTH RESEARCH CENTRE

I use a Hulda Clark-designed Zincrometer and a frequency generator Varizapper. Both of these devices I purchased from www.drclark.com. I have a large collection of testing vials from all over the world.

I have all of Hulda Clark's books, of course, and the index to her published material and speeches, which was written by David Amrein. All of these books are available at www.drclark.com, as well.

World without Cancer by Ed and Pat Griffin and all of their books and videos are inspirational; this couple has been fighting for our rights all their lives. They are wonderful people and their work should be required reading for all medical practitioners.

I cannot thank the brave pioneers in alternative health enough, especially Hulda Clark, because without her I would be dead today. In fact, many of my patients and her readers all over the world have extended their lives and improved the quality of their lives. When I read Hulda Clark's first book I was constantly thinking that what she wrote could not possibly be right. After 10 years I have not found her to be wrong about anything. Her discoveries are so revolutionary that they are difficult to accept until seen with one's own eyes. My faith in her grows as I learn. My hope is that my work can contribute to hers, and I can do my part to advance her studies and spread the word to save more lives. All of her books are available from Clarks.

Dr. David Williams' web site is very informative.

Bernard Jensen, the "Father of Naturopathy," and his book, *Health and Long Life*, were a huge influence on my life and still are. Biworld Publishers, 1975.

John Ray ND, formerly of Rarotonga, was an influence on me and many people in the Cook Islands. He was the first Naturopath that I knew of who lived there. John taught many people about nutrition and pressure point holding. When he died years ago, I started my clinic to continue his good work.

Alan E. Baklayan ND, *Parasites: The Hidden Cause of Many Diseases*. Published by Clark Zentrum is available from Clarks. 1999.

Dr. Edward Howell, *Enzyme Nutrition*. From Avery, Penguin Putnam, 1985

Graviola fruit seeds and leaves. This is a tree that is the most beneficial to health ever researched. It is from the Amazon rain forest and grows in any tropical to subtropical area. If you cannot access the fruit, seeds, or leaves naturally, it is available from www.rain-tree.com, as graviola max supplement.

Journal of National Cancer Institute, May 17, 2011, article: "Coffee prevents prostate cancer." I love coffee and always add cinnamon to it.

I use World Health Organization Guidelines for drinking water to corroborate my findings.

LEARNING ZINCROMETER TESTING

Hulda Clark's manual helped me get started, and after a great deal of practicing, I became more and more proficient. But when I taught individuals and classes to test, I found that working with saliva samples was much easier than any other method. I received samples from all over the world that I tested and wrote reports on. I saved these samples and reports for my students to test and compare their findings with mine. That way they very rapidly learned the procedure. A large array of testing samples makes for a thorough report and diagnosis. As the proficiency increases, the confidence comes with it.

I have found a few people who just could not get it; they are usually people who are tone deaf or have hearing problems. Musicians are the easiest to teach as they immediately recognize the difference between flat and resonance.

The main thing to remember is practice makes perfect. The more you do it, the better you get at it.

Some years ago I helped a young man from India with bone cancer when his uncle asked me for help. This was Paul from the Sikh temple in Hollywood, California. When the nephew was in complete remission and his tumor had collapsed, I must have been boastful about what "I" did. Paul chastised me, saying that I must consider the spiritual affect and be less scientific and clinical. Paul and the Sikh community had been praying for the healing of the young man. Since that time I try to focus on being a funnel that spiritual energy can flow through. Humility is a much better approach to healthcare: acknowledging that the caregiver is just an instrument of God, and not God himself.

I started my clinic because I did not die when I was predicted to, and had to ask the question: "Why am I still here? What is my purpose?" Most people who have a near-death experience have this same philosophical question that they must find an answer for. When I was at my desk and a patient was in front of me, my job was to do the best I possibly could for this person no matter who it was. When I was focused in this manner, the answers were on my lips immediately and I didn't always know where the answers came from. I was plugged in to the universe.

I am not a medical doctor and never will be. I am an engineer who practiced naturopathy and alternative health care. I have never been sued for wrongful death. There are more than 2,000 people in my database whom I have helped with all kinds of illness over many years. My intention is to keep helping my fellow man until I die.

HIBISCUS TEA

(Also called Jamaica Punch)

Put two heaping cups of dried hibiscus flowers and one cup of sugar in a large bowl. Pour in four cups of boiling water and stir to dissolve the sugar. Let it steep for two or three hours, then add four cups of cold water. Strain into a pitcher and serve over ice. It will keep in the refrigerator for several days. You can use more or less sugar to taste. It is delicious.

It kills mold in kidneys, reducing blood pressure.